Tales of
Old Berkshire

Tales of
Old Berkshire

~

Cecilia Millson

With Illustrations by Don Osmond

COUNTRYSIDE BOOKS
NEWBURY, BERKSHIRE

COUNTRYSIDE BOOKS
3 Catherine Road
Newbury, Berkshire

To view our complete range of books,
please visit us at
www.countrysidebooks.co.uk

ISBN 978 1 84674 244 6

Cover designed by Peter Davies, Nautilus Design
Produced through MRM Associates Ltd., Reading
Typeset by Paragon Typesetters, Queensferry
Printed by Information Press, Oxford

Acknowledgements

IT was in 1977 that Nicholas Battle invited me to write my first Tales of Old Berkshire. During the ensuing years I have enjoyed a happy association with Countryside Books and have extended my research for old tales to other counties.

I would like to thank all who have assisted me in my research over the years with special thanks to Reg. Morris, who arranged my visit to the Royal Holloway College, Judith Hunter for information concerning Richard, Duke of Cornwall's connection with Cippenham, Daphne Phillips for help with the story of the Castle Inn Scandal, and Robin Tubb for information concerning the Hocktide Ceremony.

As always the staffs of the Reading, Newbury, and Lambourn Libraries and the Newbury Weekly News have been most helpful, and I would like to acknowledge with thanks information obtained from the pages of that paper and from those of The Reading Mercury and The Berkshire Chronicle. Finally a special thanks to Don Osmond whose lively illustrations add both interest and humour to my tales.

Cecilia Millson

Contents

BARKSHIRE – The map overleaf is by Robert Morden and shows the county around 1700, before the boundary changes of the last century.

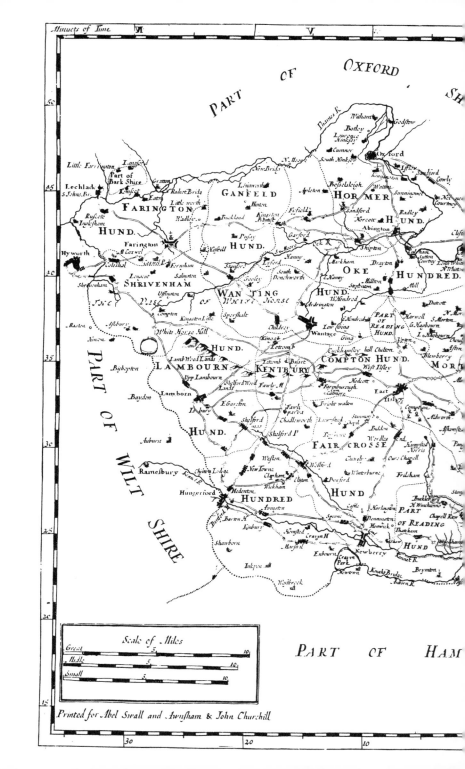

BARK SHIRE

by
Robt. Morden

PART OF BUCKINGHAM SHIRE

PART OF SURREY

SHIRE

Saved by
her Crinoline

THROUGHOUT the centuries fashion has demanded
much from women; discomfort and injury have been
endured to appease the whims of a fickle dictator.

From time to time the sheer weight of voluminous skirts
has necessitated the wearing of a frame to help a frail body
support the burden. Farthingales, panniers, and crinolines
have all been utilized. The confections of lace and satin
which covered the crinolines' steel frames, twirling to the
strains of the waltz, conjure up a picture of romance and
elegance, but many crinolines faced hazardous journeys
as their courageous owners followed their menfolk to
unknown places across the seas in an age of opportunities.

Even, more timid ladies were known to board the new
fangled trains and travel to the seaside. Alas, some never
returned. Horrific tales were told of sea-breezes suddenly
swirling across the cliffs and lifting unsuspecting ladies
high into the air to be dashed against the rocks far below.
Other poor souls were blown into the paths of galloping
horses and more than one coachman had to check his team
to save a fashionable lady from a terrible fate.

How refreshing it is in the midst of all this destruction
to know that a Reading lady owed her life to her crinoline.

Mrs Ball was the wife of a tobacconist whose shop was

situated at the junction of King's Road and Duke Street. The good lady was busy in her husband's shop one day and her horror can be imagined when, with a resounding crash, the floor gave way beneath her and she found herself falling into the void below. She landed, not on solid ground as might be expected, but in the waters of the Holy Brook which flowed beneath the shop.

Luck was with Mrs Ball that day. She fell upright and her crinoline opened out to keep her afloat as she was carried into the darkness. Terrified she may have been but she maintained her poise and was carried out into the open stream as it neared the old Abbey mill. Her loud cries attracted the attention of passers-by as they walked in the Forbury. They ran to her aid and she was quickly dragged to the safety of the bank, unharmed but very shocked, as well she might be for she was pregnant at the time of this unfortunate experience.

In due course the baby was born, and Mr and Mrs Ball decided that the name of Holybrook would be appropriate for their small son. Whether he appreciated his unusual name is doubtful. In childhood Holybrook Ball was inclined to be 'chesty' and the family had no doubt at all that this condition was due to his poor mother's untimely adventure.

Duel
for Love

FRANCES KENDRICK was born in the parish of St Mary, Reading, in the year 1687. She was the eldest daughter of a wealthy father, William Kendrick, whose family were renowned as rich cloth merchants, and great benefactors of the town.

Her grandmother had left her £5,000 a year, and added to the wealth of this fortunate young lady was a most beautiful countenance, so that her suitors were many as she grew to womanhood. The toast of Berkshire, she could take her choice.

However, aspiring husbands found no favour with the heiress. Although by nature a kindly, friendly girl, she remained aloof from their advances. But Cupid is capricious and one day, at a friend's wedding, Frances fell in love with Benjamin Child, a poor but handsome lawyer. Not that the modest young man realised that he had captured the heart of the wealthy beauty. He would have been most surprised to know that she had acquainted herself not only with his name but with the address of his lodging as well.

Her friends did not take kindly to her infatuation, but in spite of their entreaties she could not forget her lawyer.

She sat brooding about her love, weeping at not seeing him again, until she decided that she must act if he was not to pass from her life for ever. She reasoned that, as he had disturbed her peace of mind and heart, she was entitled to send him a challenge.

Thus it was that one morning Benjamin Child was shocked to receive a note challenging him to a duel. To his knowledge he had given no cause for this to happen, and he hurriedly consulted a friend. Honour demanded that he must attend the appointed place, but it was with a puzzled mind that he arrived at the park to meet his opponent. His friend had agreed to act as his second.

Benjamin Child's bewilderment grew when he was confronted, not by an angry man, but a masked lady, who inquired whom he sought. He told her of the challenge and added that, although he did not know his opponent, he was determined to show his resolve and fight.

In the words of the old ballad, 'The Berkshire Lady', she replied:

> It was I who did invite you,
> You shall wed me or I'll fight you,
> Underneath these spreading trees –
> Therefore, choose you which you please.

> You shall find I do not waver
> For here is a trusty rapier,
> So, now take your choice, said she,
> Either fight, or marry me.

If the young man was bewildered before, he was naturally overwhelmed by such a strange pronouncement, and asked the lady what she could mean, adding

14

a request that she would at least unmask. She remained adamant – he must fight or marry her, and she would not unmask until the marriage rites were over.

Benjamin Child quickly conferred with his trusted friend who pointed out that he was so poor that he had nothing to lose and might as well marry his unknown admirer, so somewhat reluctantly the lawyer consented to the wedding.

Frances Kendrick entered her coach, followed by the two young men, and they drove to the church. The bridegroom was to be allowed no time for a change of mind!

When the ceremony was over the lady, still retaining her mask, dismissed the friend after handing him a favour, and drove with her husband to her house at Calcot Park. Hand in hand they walked to a parlour where she left the bemused young man for two hours to ponder over his rash act, alone, without even the comfort of any sustaining refreshment. He had no idea, as yet, that all the beautiful apartments with their luxurious furnishings belonged to his bride.

He watched the servants pass by the open doorway, peeping at him, and he began to wish that he was back in his own humble lodging. Just as he was feeling really downcast, he was further embarrassed by the questions of the steward who was becoming suspicious of the stranger.

It was fortunate that the lady of the house appeared at that moment, having watched the proceedings through a secret peephole. Benjamin Child did not recognise the magnificently gowned beautiful woman who confronted him as his masked bride until she said:

I will be no longer cruel
To my joy and only jewel,
You are mine, and I am thine,
Hand and heart I do resign.

Once I was a wounded lover,
But now all those fears are over;
By receiving what I gave,
Thou art lord of all I have.

The bewildered young bridegroom had indeed met with good fortune – 'Beauty, honour, love and pleasure – a rich golden store of pleasure' were his reward for his trustful if rash decision.

Strange though the wooing might have been, the marriage proved all that could be desired, and Benjamin and Frances Child became the parents of two lovely daughters. Unfortunately, there was no son to carry on their family name.

It was a tragedy when Frances died at the early age of 35. In 1722 she was buried in the parish in which she was born. Her broken-hearted husband outlived his wife by 45 years. He never married again, and we can be sure that he never forgot his remarkable wedding day when he married his beautiful Berkshire Lady.

The Hazards of Early Ballooning

TODAY we frequently leave earth to fly into the sky and soar above the clouds, but 200 years ago flight was thought barely feasible by all but a few intrepid pioneers.

The first recorded successful human flight was by the Montgolfier brothers, who flew over Paris on 21st November 1783 in a hot air balloon – a container filled with air and heated by a naked flame, a mind-boggling feat of heroism for that or any time. The following month the French physicist Jacques Charles – who discovered the properties of hydrogen and the fact that gas expands with a rise in temperature (Charles's Law) made the first hydrogen balloon ascent in France. The Italian Vincenzo Lunardi ascended the English skies by hydrogen balloon from Moorfields, London, in September 1784 and the following year Jean Pierre Blanchard flew across the Channel from Dover to Calais by hot air balloon. Blanchard, incidentally, was also the inventor of the parachute – a discovery that killed him in 1809 when he jumped from a balloon.

Balloons were first used in war in 1794 by Napoleon for observation purposes; they were employed sporadically and none too effectively after that until their appearance

as barrage balloons in the Second World War.

In 1821 coal gas was first used to fill balloons as a cheap (and one would suppose, a highly dangerous) alternative to hydrogen and this opened up the possibility of balloon flight to a greater number of people, though still mainly for exhibitions, fairs, and for scientific purposes. Helium replaced hydrogen and coal gas at the end of the 19th century, after which attention was more focused on the heavier than air machines – the fore-runner of the modern aircraft. More recently ballooning is again in vogue; now as hot air balloons, carrying propane gas heaters.

But in the last few years of the 19th century flight was still an adventure experienced by few; among these the Revd John Mackenzie Bacon and his daughter Gertrude discovered the thrills and dangers of rising above the earth in a balloon.

Born on 19 June 1846, John Bacon was the son of the vicar of Lambourn Woodlands. After ten years at Cambridge University, where he was ordained, he left in 1875 because of ill-health, and moved first to North Stoke, Oxfordshire, then purchased a house, Sunnyside, in Cold Ash, near Newbury, where he lived for the remainder of his life.

Cold Ash was then a remote and neglected corner of Berkshire, and John Bacon attempted to bring cheer into the drab lives of the villagers by organising entertainments. A keen gardener, he encouraged the cottagers to cultivate their own gardens and allotments. He occasionally assisted the vicar but was more involved with St Mary's Church, Shaw, where his friend the Hon and Revd John Horatio Nelson (great-nephew of Admiral Lord Nelson) was rector.

His parochial work came to an end after he caused consternation by the publication of a pamphlet *The Curse of*

Conventionalism, a Remonstrance by a Priest of the Church of England, following this by a meeting in Newbury Town Hall to explain his views. Afterwards he preached only at the request of hard-pressed parish priests.

After the death of his wife Bacon became more involved in his most compelling interest – ballooning, which he regarded not only as a sporting occupation but as a means of furthering scientific research. He worked closely with Neville Maskelyne on his experiments with wireless telegraphy and, accompanied by his daughter Gertrude (his biographer), undertook aeronautical expeditions in Great Britain, Norway, India and America. But a flight launched from Newbury Gasworks was to prove the most dangerous of his career.

Astronomers had predicted that in the early morning hours of 16 November 1899 a shower of meteors would fall from the constellation Leo. 'Leonids' appear only once in 33 years and, after a very successful sighting in 1866, not only astronomers were enthusiastic but the public also was excited at the prospect of such an unusual sight.

The fact that November mists might obscure the skies gave Bacon the notion to take to a balloon and so ascend above the clouds, ensuring that the meteors would be seen, if only by a few aeronauts.

With financial backing from *The Times* newspaper he planned the trip. His daughter and Stanley Spencer, an experienced aeronaut were to be his companions. After consultations with Mr Spencer and his brother it was decided to replace the 'butterfly' variety of valve with a 'solid' or 'ripping' type. This decision was taken after astronomers had warned that the party should be ready to take off the night before the planned date, as the meteors might appear on the 15th. As the balloon would have to be inflated in readiness for such an eventuality there was a danger that gas might escape from a butterfly valve during such a long period of inflation, whereas a solid or ripping valve would remain completely airtight. There was one disadvantage. Once opened the latter type could not be reclosed, for the valve would rip open the balloon silk allowing gas to escape uncontrollably; so it could only be operated when the balloon was within seconds of landing. No difficulty being foreseen, the chosen valve was fitted. For technical reasons, it was decided that the voyage must be completed by dawn.

Filled with 56,000 cubic feet of coal gas the balloon was in readiness at the gasworks by the evening of Tuesday, 14th November, but the night was clear and by the early hours of the 15th November it was apparent that the meteors would not be making a premature appearance. The following night was entirely different, with thick cloud obscuring the stars. It would be impossible to see the meteors from the earth and the aeronauts felt that their journey was fully justified. Above the clouds would be the only possible viewpoint.

At midnight the three drove from Cold Ash to Newbury, fully prepared with warm clothing and all the necessary equipment to record the great event. They were welcomed by friends who had assembled at the Guildhall Club, one of Newbury's leading establishments, which was prepared to stay open all night. Four am was the time set for the ascent.

Although a light drizzle was falling as the party reached the gasworks, a large crowd had assembled as the final preparations were made. Everything that was deemed essential to the success of the voyage, was packed into the basket; even lifebelts were included in the unlikely event of a descent into the sea. A discussion took place. Were they really necessary? The lifebelts were discarded.

The great moment arrived, the gaswork's sirens sounded and the balloon rose into the darkness. As the Davy lamp, the aeronauts' only light, grew smaller the crowds slowly departed. Bacon had promised to send a telegram to the Guildhall Club as soon as possible after landing. The members little knew how long they would have to wait for that message.

As the balloon became immersed in heavy clouds its progress faltered. Ballast was thrown out as it struggled through a cloud bank 1,500 feet deep. Four sandbags were emptied before the balloon emerged and the aeronauts beheld a sight of unbelievable beauty.

Stars like jewels glittered before them. All the colours of the rainbow were caught in the light of a full moon and held against a backcloth of the deepest blue. For several moments the purpose for which they had come into this wonderland was forgotten. Then their eyes turned towards Leo — not one meteor! Their disappointment was mitigated by a sense of awe as they looked about them. Then they were recalled to reality. The balloon was sinking back into the clouds. More sandbags were emptied, making seven within a space of twenty minutes. Heavy moisture had dampened the silk to produce this unusual condition.

Bacon wanted to remain aloft for a time to complete other observations. The balloon remained steady just above the mists and 3,000 feet above the earth. All seemed well and the aeronauts were content in their fairyland, wrapped in their rugs as they enjoyed their sandwiches. They calculated their exact position from sounds rising from below. Barking dogs indicated the Ashdown Kennels, noises of a train, then horses' hooves told them that they were above the Great Western Railway line and the Bath Road. Sounds of a hooter came from the iron-works at Westbury.

The sky changed and dawn was breaking, confirmed by the crowing of cockerels far below. It was time for descent but the balloon remained aloft. No more ballast had been discharged – why was height being maintained? Gertrude Bacon inquired if it would be safe to remove the valve if height was still being maintained in half an hour but the answer was quickly in the negative. She realised that as the silk dried in the rising sun the gas would expand – they would rise, not fall. The ripping valve could not be opened. Bacon leant over the side of the balloon to look down on the cloud floor and lost his cap. In spite of their dilemma the three worried aeronauts laughed as they thought of the bewilderment of a farm labourer as he received a cap from the heavens on his way to work.

The sun rose in its glory and in its warmth the balloon rose 500 feet. It was seven o'clock – five hours before noon might bring them relief from the sun's overpowering ability to keep them afloat above the clouds. They still had sandwiches and, although cramped in the basket, conditions were bearable. It was the thought of the distance they might travel that concerned them. They were heading towards the sea, the Atlantic was waiting to receive them and they had discarded those lifebelts!

At present they were above the countryside – muffled sounds reached them as they floated above the clouds. Then, with dismay, they heard the sound of a ship's siren followed by the unmistakable clanging of hammers – they must be over the shipyards of a seaport town. The sound of waves breaking over a pebbled beach confirmed their fears. They were following the coast line, but how long remained before they were swept out to sea?

The rays of the sun became almost unbearable. Bacon knotted his handkerchief and placed it on his head – he no longer laughed at the loss of his cap. Very calmly he composed a telegram to *The Times*, then suggested that they should take photographs of the cloud floor and of one another huddled in the balloon basket. Finally, he remembered the blank telegraph forms in his pocket. Urgent messages were dropped overboard. Perhaps they would be picked up and boats launched in search of them. Anyway, it passed the time. Afterwards two of these messages were found – in Wales. Bacon worried not so much for himself but for his daughter and Stanley Spencer who was the father of two young children. No doubt driven by intense anxiety, Spencer suggested that the valve should be opened, but Bacon intervened. Better to drift to sea and be drowned than be dashed to pieces by a swift descent to earth. They drifted on, still haunted by the sound of waves. Subsequently they realised that they had drifted 20 miles over the Bristol Channel but at the time they thought only of the sea. At noon Bacon who was carefully watching the aneroid, reported that they had dropped from 9,000 feet at the last reading to 7,000 feet and were still falling.

Stanley Spencer who had been watching the cloud floor cried out that he could see a church spire. His companions feared that his mind had become confused under the unbearable strain but, sure enough, the cloud floor was parting and for a few moments they could discern a white road against a reddish background. They were over the West Country, but hopes were soon dashed as the balloon gathered speed – they could not be far from the coast.

Two hours later they finally broke through the remaining mist and saw green fields still beneath them. Now, however, they were descending all too quickly, but the aeronauts dared not release more ballast to steady the descent for fear they would rise again.

They braced themselves for the final fall. A sudden gust of wind, the remnant of a gale which had raged along the coast for days, caught the balloon, hurled it to the earth, and then dragged it along a gulley. The grapnel furrowed the ground, a barbed wire fence loomed ahead. They ducked in obedience to a command from Bacon as the strands curled round the basket. Bacon's leg was badly lacerated, his daughter's arm had been broken by the violent landing, and now before them was a withered oak tree. They crashed into it taking the top away in the balloon's rigging, but the roots of the tree held the anchor. Their journey was over. They were within five minutes, and one and a half miles, of reaching the Atlantic.

They had landed on the outskirts of Neath. Farmhands were quickly on the scene but never having seen a balloon just stood in amazement. The arrival of the landowner motivated them into helpful activity and the three travellers from the sky were soon standing on firm ground. Spencer said it was the roughest landing that he had ever made.

The following morning three dishevelled aeronauts arrived at the offices of *The Times* – still in their dirt, although Bacon had perforce borrowed a pair of trousers as his own had been torn to shreds by the barbed wire. He refused to brush the mud from his coat, his daughter's right arm was in a splint, but their reception was 'gratifying and flattering' according to Gertrude's account of their achievement. They had completed the longest flight by a balloon over Britain, narrowly escaping death, but fully determined to continue their research in the skies.

Sir Roger
Returns Home

THERE is an undoubted smile on the carved face of
the Norman knight Sir Roger de Burghfield. He may
well have been a cheerful man or, perhaps, the 14th
century woodcarver showed a sense of humour as he
worked upon the wooden effigy that was to be placed
beside the knight's tomb following his death in 1327.

Poor Sir Roger, he needed that smile as he faced the
trials that beset him during the 19th and 20th centuries
after more than 500 years of peace in the church of St
Mary the Virgin in the village of Burghfield. The de
Burghfields had held the manor under the powerful
Mortimer family since the time of Domesday, but Sir
Roger was destined to be the last of his line to do so. A
most noble knight, not only was he lord of the manor of
Burghfield but also Member of Parliament for Berkshire
in 1301, then twice Member for Oxfordshire. At the time
of his death, his brother Peter de Burghfield was the parish
priest, presumably it was he who had the effigy placed in
the church. It is a remarkable example of 14th century
English wood carving, probably executed in London but
showing signs of French influence, particularly in the
skilled carving of the costume of the period.

After having lain in the church for five centuries it is

incredible that when the church was rebuilt in 1843 the effigy was placed ignominiously under the belfry stairs. There Sir Roger remained until 1931 when, during renovation work, he was discovered and reinstalled in a specially built recess near the High Altar. But fate intervened once more to wrest Sir Roger from his resting place. In January 1978 parishioners were appalled to hear that the effigy had been stolen from the church. Who the culprits were and how they managed to smuggle it out of the country is still a mystery, but three months later it appeared at an antique fair in Ghent, Belgium. Apparently it had passed through various hands but had been bought in good faith by a dealer who put it up for sale at the fair as a 15th century Flemish effigy. A London dealer, who did not accept this description, made further research and coming to the conclusion that the effigy was that of Sir Roger de Burghfield contacted the vicar.

The parishioners were overjoyed to know that the effigy was found but four years of negotiations and fund raising were to take place before they could welcome it home. Firstly, for six months the effigy was placed into the custody of the Court of Bruges which eventually decided that, under Belgian law, the new owner must be compensated by at least £4,000, the sum he had paid for it. Joy turned to dismay when the people of Burghfield were told of the court's ruling but worse news was to follow.

It was calculated that by the time the compensation was paid, plus legal and other costs, plus the expense of procuring a secure cabinet for Sir Roger, nearly £10,000 would be needed. A daunting thought but parishioners were determined to have their effigy back and an appeal was launched. Donations were sent from all parts of the United Kingdom as well as from overseas but it was mainly by parochial efforts that the huge sum was raised.

The spirit of determination which prevailed in the village was epitomised by the pensioner who, when presenting a modest but precious donation, declared that it was 'to help bring Sir Roger back home where he belongs'. How values change! An effigy that was relegated to a position under the stairs by Victorian parishioners in 1843 was so highly prized by their descendants some 140 years later that £10,000 was raised to regain it, not only as a village but as a national treasure.

In May 1982 the effigy was replaced in the church and a thanksgiving service was held for Sir Roger's safe return. He is now enclosed in a steel and armoured glass cabinet – and he is still smiling.

The Lonely
Gibbet
of Combe

MEN have walked along the hill tracks of Inkpen since time immemorial. They travelled above the swamps and forests as they roamed in search of food even before the Iron Age fort of Walbury brought some measure of security to themselves and their flocks.

Now, the hills are a favourite picnic place and walkers, cyclists, and motorists make their way up the steep inclines on any fine day, and children (and their fathers) run with their kites which are carried high by the strong breeze. They spare a moment to gaze upon the gibbet; then on again before the kites drop to the ground.

The rush of life is halted for a brief spell as everyone admires the magnificent views all around – quiet farmsteads, fields, and woodlands, where once thick forests stood.

As the evening haze falls over the hills the visitors depart, leaving the gibbet to face the dark night and await the coming of winter, when buffeted by strong winds and swirling snow it stands alone. For more than three hundred years Combe Hill has been dominated by this grim reminder of past misdeeds.

Over the years the tales surrounding the gibbet have passed from father to son, varying sometimes in the telling, but always naming George Broomham and Dorothy Newman as the two criminals who swung from that first gibbet in 1676.

The most accepted story is that George Broomham was a labourer who lived at the nearby hamlet of Combe with his wife Martha, and his son, Robert.

Unfortunately, George became infatuated with Dorothy Newman of Inkpen, who encouraged his advances. Eventually, they decided to murder poor Martha and Robert and so remove any hindrance to their own alliance.

They laid their plans carefully, and waited for a suitable opportunity to carry out their wicked deed. It came one day when Martha decided to walk over the lonely hill accompanied by her young son. As they came over the crest they were set upon and savagely beaten to death with cudgels wielded by George Broomham and Dorothy Newman, who were to pay dearly for their crime.

The couple were arrested and appeared at the Winchester Assizes in February, 1676. Found guilty, it was decreed that they should be 'hanged in chaynes near the place of the murder'. The execution took place the following month, the only time the gibbet was used for such a purpose.

None of the principals who took part in that tragic drama could have foreseen that 270 years later they would be the subject of a film.

With local people as actors and actresses, it was written and directed by Alan Cooke and John Schlesinger, then on the threshold of his career as a film director. I saw the film in 1948 and again a few years ago. It captures the atmosphere of that remote part of Berkshire which was shattered by the horror of scandal and murder in the midst of its peace and security. The film is justly called *'The Black Legend'*.

The original gibbet has long since rotted away. Replacements have been destroyed by lightning, gales, and vandalism, but always another one has been erected on the hill top, so determined are the local people to commemorate the sad story of long ago.

The Amazing Journey of William Bush of Lambourn

TO TRAVEL by air, land, and water may be an easy achievement nowadays but at the beginning of the seventeenth century it seemed but a fantastic dream. Yet men tried again and again to bring that dream to reality.

William Bush was one man who succeeded for, 'by his cunning and skill Mathematique and Geometrical', he designed a small boat of the pinnace class, which he constructed very carefully with his own hands, allowing no other man to help him. In this vessel he managed to travel by air, land, and water from Lambourn to the Customs House Quay in London, and we are indebted to his friend 'A.N.' who recorded in detail the exploits of the gallant inventor.

On the morning of Monday, the twentieth day of July, 1607, William Bush brought forth his masterpiece from the house of his friend, William Essex, Esquire, of Lambourn. What he had not taken into account was the enthusiasm of hundreds of people who waited to greet him.

The news of the elaborate preparations in the churchyard had been carried far and wide. Surrounding farms must have been devoid of labour, markets deserted, and cottages empty if 'A.N.' has not exaggerated the numbers who were present on that day.

Many had never seen a boat before and they gazed in wonder at the little pinnace, complete with oars and 'four mastes and yardes of the most fine light timber that might be had or procured'. That was not all, 'she had twelve pieces of Ordinance in her, that went off by a strange device in just order, one after the other; they were planted on a platforme framed for that purpose uppon the Tower-decks in their equall proportions, and no man neere them at their discharging'.

To say that the ship was dressed overall is to under-estimate the enthusiasm of her owner; she carried 'flagges, aunciens, streamers, and pendents of rich Taffetie, the colours sable and argent, according to the colours of him that made and framed her; her several flagges were beautified with divers Coates of Armes, as the Armes of England, the Essex coate, the Harcourts, and the Waynemans: and the coate of the Shippewright, and his ancestors, with divers other Gentlemen of worthe, and worship in that country . . .'

A stout platform had been built on top of the tall tower of Lambourn Church; another in the churchyard below 'fastened deepe in the earth with windlasses and other Engins to strain the ropes and assist the Pynace in moving by other devices'.

Two strong cables, nearly sixty five yards in length and weighing one hundredweight each were fastened to the tower platform 'with windlasses and other devices in it'.

The cables ran down one hundred feet apart (the width of the pinnace) and were secured to two stout trees.

34

So, when all was set in motion, the pinnace could be persuaded 'to move by degrees, either ascending or descending'.

William Bush certainly deserved every jot of admiration which was bestowed upon him by his friends – all that effort for a journey of 'three score yardes'.

The intense interest of the crowd was to prove a hindrance to the eager traveller. Nearly an hour passed before the pinnace could be brought to the ground platform and settled upon the cables, but soon she was ready to begin her ascent to the top of the tower. No one was aboard for that first voyage and as the little boat descended gasps of astonishment greeted the firing of her guns and the display of fireworks and other strange devices, for there was nobody within twenty feet of her to set these wonders in motion.

It was hoped that the free display would satisfy the people, for William Bush planned to start his real voyage the next day. However, the crowds refused to disperse and demanded to see a man aboard. William Bush, fearing damage to his craft went on board himself, and once again the pinnace was airborne, to the satisfaction of the two thousand people below.

It was nearly six o'clock when the air-boat was returned to the safety of Mr Essex's garden.

If Mr Bush thought to slip away quietly the next morning he was sadly mistaken. The crowd was greater than before, which is proof that it was possible to take two days off from work in those bad old days! It took twenty men to force a passage through the crowd and to set it up on the launching platform. Forty feet in the air she was suspended, out of harm's way, while the inventor checked that all was in order. Then the boat was brought down and he ascended to the top of the tower, but one danger he had not foreseen. Unbeknown to him, some seventy men, women, and children had climbed the tower to gain a viewpoint from the roof. They clung to the pinnacles, the ropes, the pullies, even to the iron bracket of the weather vane, and they disregarded all danger in order to see the ascent of the pinnace. The extra weight took its toll. As the boat started to move with her commander on board, the two main pinnacles fell down into the tower amongst the people who were standing there. By a miracle no one was hurt by the falling masonry. Panic reigned until someone had the forethought to call from the tower that all were safe, but the accident brought the foolish people hurrying down to ground level.

William Bush, having given thanks to God for the safe deliverance of the people, left his boat and went into the tower to see if any equipment had been damaged. He was satisfied that all was well and prepared to embark again in spite of pleas from his friends to remain safely on the ground. He pointed out that in truth God was with him on the adventure and with a cheerful countenance was hauled to the top of the tower. He gravely saluted his friends and then 'by his owne industrie and labour let himself downe by degrees to the ground to the joy and wonder of all the beholders'. The journey by air was safely accomplished.

Now the journey by land must commence and the boat was put on 'wheels and divers other Engyns' which were placed in readiness at the lower end of the ropes. Having made ready, Mr Bush sat in his wonderful machine and passed to and fro in the churchyard to see that all was well appointed for his journey. He travelled only to his friend's house that night for he was vexed and troubled by the hindrance of the crowd and was persuaded to rest before pursuing his journey.

Between four and five o'clock on Wednesday afternoon he was finally prepared and travelled from Lambourn to Up-Lambourn, a distance of roughly a quarter of a mile. As it was then seven o'clock in the evening he ceased his labour for that day and rested the whole of Thursday, setting out again on Friday afternoon.

He needed to be well refreshed for he had to ascend 'an exceeding high hill towards Childerie downes, which he could very hardly attain the top of, but with great enforcement of paines and labour'. Downhill was easy and so overjoyed was Mr Bush that he mistakenly attempted the ascent of another steep incline. This almost proved too much for him, but, having conquered it, he left his boat under guard and returned to Lambourn for a night's rest.

Recovered, he rejoined the boat and went from Childrey Downs to the lodge of Sir Edmund Fettiplace on Saturday. There is no mention of any travel on Sunday, but on Monday he covered a distance of five miles and reached Carmislow Hill. His progress the next day was disappointing. An important key by which the pinnace was guided and governed broke suddenly and reduced his distance to only one mile, but he achieved five miles again on Wednesday, reaching Aldworth. He concluded his journey, coming to Streatley and the Thames, on Thursday.

Now came the final test. Mr Bush watched anxiously as his boat settled on the water but she stood the test having been 'very carefully calked and pitched to keep the water forth'. All seemed well, but now the worst misadventure of the journey befell poor William Bush.

A gang of bargemen waded into the water and started to destroy the strange craft. In vain they were entreated to stop their vandalism. They responded to the pleas with abuse and coarse laughter. Mr Bush and his two companions were hopelessly outnumbered. Although the commander was unhurt his attendants were badly injured and to save their lives he removed them to the safety of their lodgings, leaving his precious boat to the mercy of the ruffians. Maliciously they rent her with pike staves and long hooks until they thought the little pinnace was damaged beyond repair, but they had reckoned without the courage and indomitable spirit of William Bush.

He mended his craft and on August 19th he set course for London where he arrived safely at the Customs Quay and was greeted by the Customer, Controller, and Surveyor. They willingly agreed to issue a certificate confirming that the voyage had been made when entreated to do so by the witnesses who had accompanied the intrepid adventurer. Mr Bush and his company were graciously entertained by all the officers and feasted at the Customer's house.

William Bush had achieved his ambition, but the tower of Lambourn Church bore the scars of his adventure.

The two northern pinnacles show signs of seventeenth-century repairs but it was not until the restoration work of 1891-92 that the real damage was discovered. A crack nearly three and a half inches wide ran through the whole thickness of the north wall, no doubt due to the strain imposed upon it at the commencement of that incredible journey – 'Threescore yardes in the Ayre, Six and Twentie myles uppon the Land, and an hundreth myles uppon the water'.

The Wokingham Beauty

WHEN the early 18th century landlord of the Rose Inn at Ockingham (Wokingham) welcomed a party of diners to his inn he little thought that by their pens his daughter's name would become a household word, not only in Berkshire but far beyond the county's borders.

John Mogg knew his customers well. Alexander Pope lived at Binfield and would frequently call at the inn with his friends, Dean Swift, John Gay, and Dr Arbuthnot, but on this particular occasion they stayed longer than usual, detained by a violent storm.

To while away the time they wrote verses to Molly, one of the landlord's two beautiful daughters. John Gay is thought to have been the chief author of the ballad but Pope and Swift probably contributed some of the lines. Dr Arbuthnot seems to be a doubtful collaborator as some versions of the story do not acknowledge his presence on that afternoon.

The first verse introduces the love-sick admirer and names the cause of his dejection:

> Says my Uncle, I pray you discover
> What had been the cause of your woes
> Why you pine and whine like a lover?
> I've seen Molly Mog of the Rose.

The next thirteen verses sing her praises and tell of the young man's obsession with his love. To quote but one:

A letter when I am inditing
Comes Cupid and gives me a jog,
And I fill all the paper with writing
Of nothing but Sweet Molly Mog.

The final verse tells of his consuming jealousy and the apparent hopelessness of his suit:

While she smiles on each guest like her liquor
Then jealousy sets me agog,
To be sure she's a bit for the Vicar,
And so I shall lose Molly Mog.

One can imagine the laughter and sallies as the verses were composed by gentlemen who had dined and wined well at the old inn.

There was obviously scant sympathy for the forlorn young man. He is thought to be Edward Standen of Arborfield, the last male heir of the manor which had been held by his family since 1589. He died in 1730 at the age of 27.

The ballad first appeared in *Mist's Weekly Journal* under the title 'Molly Mog, or the Fair Maid of the Inn.' It was noted 'that it was writ by two or three men of wit, upon the occasion of their lying at a certain Inn at Ockingham, where the daughter of the House was remarkably pretty, and whose name was Molly Mog.' (*Oxford Companion of English Literature* 1940.)

The fair lady's name also figured in a Welsh ballad:

> Some sing Molly Mogg of the Rose
> And call her the Ockingham belle
> Whilst others does ferses compose
> On beautiful Molly Lapelle.

One wonders if the young lady in question became embarrassed by the publicity, but undoubtedly it was good for business as it attracted customers to the inn. Molly's sister was reputed to be even more attractive and it has been suggested that the ballad referred to Sarah, or Sally, and not to her elder sister. But Alexander Pope would have known the landlord's daughters well and would have been unlikely to confuse the two sisters.

In spite of her beauty Molly Mogg remained a spinster to the end of her days. She outlived her parents and her brother and sister and died at the age of 67 on Sunday, 9th March 1766. The record of her death describes her as 'Mrs. Mary Mogg, advanced in years but in her youth a celebrated beauty and toast, possessed of a good fortune that she has left among her relations'.

Apparently her brother had two daughters and no son so that on the death of Mary, or Molly, Mogg the family name died with her. It was a strange name but one made famous as those noted wits toyed with words on a stormy afternoon.

Berkshire Fairs

EAST OR MARKET ILSLEY
AN IMPORTANT
TRADING CENTRE SINCE THE 13th CENTURY
WAS GRANTED A ROYAL CHARTER IN 1620.
ON THIS SITE WERE HELD THE SHEEP FAIRS
WHICH IN IMPORTANCE WERE SECOND ONLY
TO SMITHFIELD AND WERE HELD FORTNIGHTLY
FROM APRIL TO OCTOBER.
THE LAST ONE WAS HELD IN 1934

THIS inscription on a wayside plaque in the centre of East Ilsley is a reminder of times when the village was thronged with sheep and its 24 inns and public houses were frequented by the farmers, drovers, and shepherds who came to the fortnightly sales.

Since prehistoric times men have travelled the Berkshire Downs, and ancient tracks lead down to this village which was a trading centre even before it became famous for its sheep fairs.

The charter of 1620, granted by James I, gave royal approval to the great sheep fair held at the end of July or beginning of August. This continued to be the most important of the many fairs held in East Ilsley. As many as 80,000 sheep were penned in the village on one occasion during the 19th century. Throughout the year an average sale was around 400,000 sheep. The pens lined the sides of the street and trees were planted to provide shade for the animals as they waited patiently for the highest bidders to become their new owners. The noise and bustle must have been tremendous at the fortnightly sales when men, sheep and dogs thronged the roads. In between the fairs East Ilsley retained its unusual appearance with the empty pens standing row upon row along the village street but these short breaks must have given the inhabitants welcome spells of peace – except, perhaps, the landlords of the inns!

Cosburn's directory of 1901 lists 18 fairs at East Ilsley during that year, of which 27th March was a fair for both sheep and cattle, 10th April, the Easter fair, 29th May the Whitsun fair, and 13th October the hiring fair. At this last, if they so wished, shepherds, farm hands and servants changed their employment for the coming year.

J.E. Vincent, writing in the *Highways and Byways of Berkshire* at the beginning of the century, gave a word of warning to cyclists, and the few motorists of those days, who were likely to visit East Ilsley. He wrote of the chalk and flint roads, leading to the village from Steventon in the north, or from Compton to the east. Although normally not bad roads, when the flocks of sheep had passed over them the surface was destroyed and the little flints were churned up to stand as sharp as swords, to the detriment of tyres. Mr Vincent had evidently needed to mend a puncture when he travelled the byways to the fair. It was the introduction of modern transport which finally caused the decline of the sheep sales. The drovers no longer had to walk their animals to the country markets.

There is a lovely tale of days gone by. When a shepherd died a piece of sheep's wool would be placed in his coffin as proof of his calling. He could then convince St Peter that there was good reason for his irregular church attendance. At times his sheep needed him even on the Sabbath day, and as a good shepherd he could never neglect his flock.

It was the woollen trade which brought prosperity to Newbury, not by the sale of sheep, but in the making of their wool into fine cloth, and Newbury, too, had its ancient fairs.

The first fair was granted on the 7th July 1215 by King John so that provision could be made for the St Bartholomew's Hospital, or almshouses, which he had founded. Appropriately, the fair was held on the day and morrow of the feast of St Bartholomew, apostle and martyr (24th August).

Later, Edward IV granted two four-day fairs, one on the eve and feast of Corpus Christi and two days following, and the other on the eve and feast of the Nativity of St John the Baptist and two days following. The townspeople did not like these rather lengthy fairs when they lost their trade to the beneficiary of the event. The profits from these two fairs were shared, two thirds going to the crown and the other third to the King's 'trusty and beloved servant, Thomas Herbert, the elder,' in recognition of his 'good, gratuitous, and laudable service'. Unfortunately, it is not known what Thomas Herbert did to receive such a favour from the King.

When Queen Elizabeth I granted the Charter of Incorporation to the Borough of Newbury in 1596, four fairs were granted annually, on the day of the Annunciation (25th March), on the Nativity of St John the Baptist (24th June), on St Bartholomew's day (24th August) and St Simon's and St Jude's day (28th October). These fairs were entitled to their own courts of Pie Powder, derived from *Pieds Poudreux* – the court of the travellers (or men with dusty feet) whereby justice could be administered on the spot to prevent any delay in the settlement of a transaction, or before the traveller went on his way. These fairs seem to have prospered judging by the increase in their profits and tolls. Newbury, on the crossroads from London to Bath and from Southampton to the North, was a good place to trade and the fairs became widely known and used for the sale and the purchase of cattle, cheese, and other commodities.

Around 1687 the Mayor and Corporation of Newbury fell into trouble by changing the venue of the fair of St Simon and St Jude from the town site to one on Wash Common on the outskirts of Newbury. The townspeople complained to the King, and the mayor, Francis Cox, was summoned before James II and his Privy Council to explain the reason for the move, with the result that he was ordered to return the fair to its original venue, although he was granted permission to hold a sheep fair separately on the common land known as West Fields.

The origin of another fair, the Statute or Michaelmas Fair is obscure. As a Statute Fair it was probably granted by statute or ordinance of the corporation as lords of the manor and not by royal grant or licence (*History of Newbury* by Walter Money). This would date its origin sometime after 1627, the year in which the corporation became the lords of the manor of Newbury. It is known that it was in existence before 1752 as an official announcement was made regarding a slight change of date for the Hiring Fair due to the change in the calendar.

It became a very popular fair and one in which those seeking employment made their way to the Market Place or the Wharf, where the fair was held, and displayed an emblem of their calling. A shepherd would wear a piece of sheep's wool, a carter a length of whipcord, a cowman a piece of cowhair while a cook would carry a spoon and a maid a small mop. A prospective employer would thus distinguish the type of servant he needed and try to strike a bargain of employment for the coming year. If there was any difficulty about the signing of the bond by an illiterate man or woman, a cross would do, or alternatively, the acceptance of a shilling by the servant sealed the agreement.

In 1893 the Newbury corporation took steps to abolish the hiring fair. A change of attitude towards the method by which servants were engaged was making the practice of hiring at fairs unacceptable. However, there was so much opposition from some sections of the community that it was decided to hold a postal ballot to decide the matter. The result showed that most people agreed with the corporation but, at the same time, they wanted the fair to continue as an amusement fair.

While the four ancient Newbury fairs gradually fell into disuse, the Michaelmas fair grew in popularity but its growth did cause problems in the streets, especially as the traffic increased year by year. In 1945 it was decided that the time had come to move it to Northcroft, an open space near the town, and there it is still held, as well attended as ever. The mayor opens the fair and invites the children to join in the initial free rides. They scramble with enthusiasm on the gigantic brightly lit amusements – a far cry from the simple attractions provided by the showmen with the 'dusty feet'.

Reading's first fair was granted by Henry I to the Abbey which he founded in the town in 1121. He gave the Abbot and Convent the right to hold the fair on the feast of St Laurence (10th August) and the three days following.

His grandson, Henry II, added another favour, the grant of a fair on the feast of St James (25th July) and the three days following, and stated that his 'fair peace was to protect those at the fair and those going to and returning from it'. A warning to those who might be displeased at this further grant to the Abbey at the local traders' expense, as well as to any who might be tempted to try highway robbery on the merchants who did business at the fair.

In 1206 yet another fair was granted to the Abbey by King John, a frequent visitor to Reading. This was to be on the vigil and feast of St Philip and St James (1st May) and the three days following so that thirteen days of tolls, profits, and fines from these important and lucrative fairs provided revenue for the Abbey.

By 1315 the weekly market which had been held from time immemorial at a certain place, probably St Mary Butts, was moved nearer the Abbey gates by order of the Abbot. This caused the burgesses to complain to the King, Edward II, but notwithstanding an order to the sheriff to look into the matter, the market continued to be held in the area which eventually became known as the Market Place.

However, there was some consolation for the town traders. The fair around St Laurence's feast fell into disuse and had disappeared before the middle of the 15th century. The other two fairs continued to do well and were favourite venues for the settlement of debts. It was essential that this should be done when witnesses were at hand, as a written record of such a transaction was rare in the days when few people could read or write, and a professional scribe was not always available.

With the dissolution of the monasteries the tolls and profits of the two fairs were given to Sir William Penyson but later transferred to the Duke of Somerset when his nephew, Edward VI, granted him the manor, borough and fairs of Reading. When the duke fell into disgrace the gift was forfeited to the Crown.

On 23rd September 1560, Queen Elizabeth I granted Reading a new charter to restore the then decayed town to prosperity. In addition to the two existing fairs, the corporation was given permission to hold two more four day fairs, one on the feast of St Matthew (21st September) and the other on the Purification of the Blessed Virgin Mary (2nd February). All had their own courts of Pie Powder.

The four fairs were still being held in the 19th century although justice was administered through the normal channels by that time. Certain rules were drawn up for behaviour at fairs and markets, including one against drunkenness and disorderly behaviour.

Early in the 19th century John Howard Hinton, a Baptist minister, used the Forbury Cheese Fair to speak in favour of total abstinence. He was the first man in Reading to speak out in public on the matter, a brave action as some who frequented the fairs were not noted for sobriety and could have well shown resentment at his remarks.

Trade was brisk at these fairs. Those held in February, May, and July, dealt mainly in the sale of horses, cattle, and pigs and the one in July became so successful that it had to be transferred from sites in Broad Street and Friar Street to the open space of the Forbury in 1840.

The Michaelmas Fair was held there already. Cattle and horses were sold at this fair but originally it was used mainly for the sale of hops, serges, and cheese. During the 18th century it became one of the most important cheese fairs in the country and attracted producers from Somerset, Gloucester, Wiltshire, and Dorset. The highest quantity recorded at the fair was in 1795 when 1,200 tons of cheese were pitched for sale in the Forbury. Waggons which had delivered the cheese were laden with birch brooms to be sold in the towns on the homeward journey.

It was the opening of the Great Western Railway in 1840 which heralded the decline of this prosperous fair. When the produce was brought by rail rather than by road or the canal, the cheeses were not unloaded but left in the station while samples only were taken to the fair. The cheeses were then sold direct from the railway station.

The Michaelmas Fair was also a hiring fair and, as at Newbury, there were many seeking employment who displayed the tokens of their trade.

In addition to the main sales, stalls laden with household commodities, trinkets, and country produce tempted the housewives to buy while their husbands dealt with the major purchases.

It was not all business. The fairs provided plenty of amusements and people were in holiday mood. Peepshows, booths, swings and roundabouts were packed into any available space, and cheap-jacks and gipsies peddled their wares. Wombwell's menagerie was one of the chief attractions but those who participated in the business or fun of the fair needed to be wary, as the Earl of Abingdon's steward found to his cost in 1814. He had been given £240 with which to buy grey horses but a pickpocket relieved him of the money before he had made his purchase. Human nature had not changed since the days when Henry II granted his 'fair peace' to protect those who went to Reading fair.

Although the market continues, the days of the great fairs has passed, but in their time they contributed both to the prosperity and pleasure of many people, and those who had enjoyed them never regretted that they had obeyed the call to 'Come to the Fair!'

The Eccentric Baronet of Windsor

MANY MEN have gone to great lengths to win rich wives but few can claim such a record as Sir John Dineley-Goodere, the Poor Knight of Windsor. This great eccentric was the second son of Samuel Goodere of Monmouthshire. Samuel, captain of the man-of-war *Ruby,* had an elder brother, a baronet, Sir John Dineley-Goodere of Burhope in Wellington, Herefordshire. No love existed between the two brothers, and as their relationship deteriorated the baronet, who had no surviving children, announced that he intended to disinherit Samuel in favour of a nephew, John Foote of Truro, Cornwall. This was too much for Samuel who immediately planned to stop such an outrageous act.

Before the baronet had time to put his threat into action Captain Goodere arranged for him to be kidnapped in Bristol. He was then taken aboard the *Ruby* where he was murdered by two sailors on the night of Sunday, 18th January 1740. However the crime was discovered; Samuel Goodere and his two accomplices were hanged at Bristol the following April.

Thus Edward, Samuel's eldest son, inherited his uncle's title and estates, but when he died insane in March 1761 at the age of 32, they passed to his younger brother, John.

The new baronet lost little time in disposing of what remained of the family fortune and he was forced to sell Burhope in 1770. Fortunately he had some influential friends who procured for him the pension and residence of a Poor Knight of Windsor although he hardly fulfilled the original requirements for members of that Order. They were elderly soldiers of gentle birth who were appointed to St George's Chapel, Windsor, by Edward III in 1348 to pray for the Sovereign and the Garter Knights. (Since 1833 they have been known as the Military Knights of Windsor and are selected on account of their distinguished military service to be the local representatives of the Knights of the Garter at services in St George's Chapel.)

Not surprisingly Sir John discarded the disgraced name of Goodere and from then onwards was known only by the name of Dineley. However, he had no intention of fading into obscurity. Quite the reverse, for he made sure that he was noticed as he went about the historic town.

His eccentric behaviour and conspicuous style of dress made him the talk of Windsor. He left his securely locked house, to which no one was admitted, very early in the morning to purchase his meagre provisions. His dress was of the period of 30 years before. A large cloak, called a requelaure, was worn over an embroidered coat, a silk flowered waistcoat and faded velvet breeches. His thin legs were encased in a dirty pair of silk stockings. Dingy silver buckles adorned his half polished shoes, and pattens were worn if the streets were muddy. A formidable umbrella was carried as a further precaution against inclement weather, and a cocked hat and scantily powdered wig completed his day-to-day attire. For more important outings he wore a gold laced hat (the lace was rather tarnished) and a freshly powdered best wig.

One obsession now dominated Sir John's life. This was the dream of influential family connections of ancient origin, and the wealth that would be his if he could establish the authenticity of his claim. However, to do this he needed money. As far as he could see there was only one way of obtaining this elusive commodity and that was by making an advantageous marriage. It all seemed so simple to him. Surely some rich woman would like to be married to a baronet even if her affection for him personally was but slight?

His strange appearance attracted many sidelong glances from the ladies. Sir John was quick to distinguish the derisive from those of more sober interest. He disregarded any giggling females but approached, with great dignity, any lady whom he deemed worthy of his attention.

In his capacious pockets Sir John carried many leaflets, printed in his own hand, which set out his marriage proposals. Some were embellished by a suitable verse of romantic poetry. With a most courtly bow he approached the chosen lady and presented her with a copy of his proposal so that she might study it at her leisure.

It was not only in Windsor that he looked for a bride. Two or three times a year he would visit London and place advertisements in the fashionable daily papers so that the ladies would know when he intended to visit Vauxhall or the theatres. He was convinced that they would flock to meet him, and he was not entirely disappointed. Curiosity is a wonderful incentive – but there the interest ceased. The honour of marrying Sir John Dineley did not tempt any lady to part with the money he required for such matrimonial bliss.

Lack of success did not daunt him. He persisted in his

quest. Everything was planned on a sound commercial basis. He even had a sliding scale. The younger the lady, the less he demanded. However, he needed at least £100 to start his research so that was the lowest figure – for a lady of under 21 years. For a lady of more advanced age the fee was higher but whoever accepted his hand might one day share his fortune. This tempting offer fell on deaf ears.

Sir John persevered quite seriously until the end of his life, but without success. He died a bachelor in 1809 at the age of 80, and was buried in St George's Chapel. At his death the baronetcy became extinct and the Poor Knight's claim to family fame and fortune remained but a dream.

From a Country Churchyard

CHURCHYARD memorials provide an interesting study for those who care to browse round 'God's acre'. Were the departed really as virtuous as their relatives would have us believe, or were the sentimental verses chosen from a book thoughtfully provided by the monumental masons? This frequently occurred but, no doubt, some epitaphs were specially composed to do honour to the deceased or to tell the story of their demise.

The workmates of Henry West were obviously shocked and distressed when the young man was killed while working at Reading railway station in 1840, and with genuine grief erected a monument over his grave in the churchyard of St Lawrence's Church.

IN MEMORY OF HENRY WEST
Who lost his life in a WHIRLWIND at the
GREAT WESTERN RAILWAY STATION, READING
on the 24th. of March, 1840 – Aged 24 Years.
Sudden the change. I in a moment fell
and had not time to bid my friends farewell
Yet hushed be all complaint, tis sweet, tis blest,
to change Earth's stormy scenes for Endless Rest.
Dear friends prepare, take warning by my fall,
so shall you hear with joy your Saviour's call.

The wooden monument or 'rail' which marks his grave has been renewed three times, in 1862 by his brother George, in 1924 by his niece F. G Rixon, and in 1971 by the Reading Corporation. It stands by the footpath leading from the Forbury to Blagrave Street, and serves as a reminder of the terror which swept through Reading on that Tuesday afternoon as well as a memorial to the unfortunate young man who was struck down so suddenly.

The *Reading Mercury* reported 'the whole neighbourhood of Friar Street was alarmed by a loud noise resembling the crashing of heavy timber the rolling of thunder. This noise was found to have originated at the Station.' Apparently a violent gust of wind struck the railway station where several men were erecting a large shed next to the station house 'to provide for the comfort of passengers'. Although others were injured, Henry West was the only fatal casualty. He was working on the lantern, a large wooden structure on top of the building which was to provide light for the waiting room. Although it weighed four tons it was carried over the station house by the force of the wind. It damaged a chimney and then fell to the ground. Henry West was found 200 yards away. He was carried to the Boar's Head in Friar Street but death had been instantaneous.

A monument in a country churchyard was designed with considerable thought for the future. It was erected in 1855 to commemorate Job Lousley of the Manor House, Hampstead Norreys, whose generosity to his dependants made him a well loved lord of the manor. Not only is the monument itself unusual but the story behind its erection must be unique.

Job Lousley had expressed a wish to be buried on his own land in Beech Wood. Hurried consultation took place with the Bishop of Oxford but permission was refused for the use of this unorthodox site and Job Lousley was laid to rest in the churchyard in July 1855. When it was decided to erect a large monument over his grave his tenantry participated in a most practical manner.

The wives of his tenant farmers and farmworkers gathered together broken ploughshares and pieces of other farm implements. So anxious were they to help to show their regard for a man who had been helpful to them that they were able to send two cartloads of metal to Bucklebury foundry. After it was melted down it was used to erect a cast iron monument. It rises tier by tier, rather like a huge wedding cake, and is surmounted by an obelisk. As members of the Lousley family have joined their ancestor in the family tomb their names have been added on panels which are fixed to the sides of the tiers.

The last name is that of Conrad Offa Lousley who died on 9th November 1962. He was the ninth and last surviving child of Luke, eldest son of Job Lousley. After a long career in India he retired to Bradfield in Berkshire and at his death was taken back to his native village for burial with his family.

In spite of being unable to comply with his father's last wish, Luke Lousley did his best to make amends. He placed a granite memorial on the place in Beech Wood where his father used to stand to gaze over the manorial lands which he farmed and loved so well.

There is a memorial to a vastly different type of man in the churchyard of St Michael and All Angels at Lambourn. It tells its own story:

Here
lies the body
of JOHN CARTER
of this parish, labourer,
who in the defiance of the laws
of God and man
wilfully and maliciously
set fire in two places
to this town of Lambourn
on the 19th day of November 1832
and was executed at Reading
in the 30th. year of his age
on the 16th. day of March, 1833
having desired that his body
might be interred here as a
warning to his companions
and others who may hereafter
read this memorial to his
untimely end.
The wages of sin is death.
Repent and turn yourselves from
all your transgressions and so iniquity
shall not be your ruin.

One wonders if John Carter did truly express the wish that such a memorial should be erected, or whether it was the outcome of a pious hope of those responsible for its erection that the wording might deter others from committing such a futile act of folly.

An 18th century monument in the churchyard of All Saints, Wokingham, provides ample space for the recording of family history. Benjamin Beaver used a large rectangular block of Portland stone to mark the graves of his wife, Elizabeth, and their nephew, Thomas Leach. On one side is inscribed:

> Erected for the lasting remembrance of one
> of the best women who deserved more than
> I can say of her and for whose sake I have engaged
> part of my estate to keep up this monument in
> repair to the end of time.

A suitable verse extolling her many virtues accompanies this inscription.

Also recorded is a tragic event which grieved both Mr and Mrs Beaver some 26 years before her death.

> Stop youth. Take warning for here lieth also
> the remains of their beloved nephew Thomas Leach
> who was lost July 14th 1761 in swimming
> in the river Thames, near Caversham Lock, to the great
> sorrow of all who knew him. In the 16th year of his age.

With these two epitaphs one side of the monument was complete. But in order to fill the remaining three sides Benjamin Beaver then set about the task of recording the family history from the time of Charles I.

The misfortunes caused by the Civil War took pride of place. A certain Richard Beaver was a loyal supporter of King Charles and, at his own expense, raised and trained a troop of horse to serve his royal master. His brother-in-law, Sir Richard Harrison of Hurst, raised two troops, and together they joined with other friends in the neighbourhood to fight beside the King. They suffered heavily for this loyalty. It is recorded that Richard Beaver, Alexander Troughton and the family of the deceased Algernon Sime, suffered persecution and the sequestration of their estates and goods by Parliament.

Alexander Troughton's son-in-law, Thomas Bowden, also paid a high price for serving his sovereign. He was a coal merchant who supplied the court at Windsor. One can imagine the amount of fuel needed to give some semblance of warmth in that great castle. With the defeat of the King the bills were not paid and it is stated that 'he lost his Debt of Thousands by the unfortunate King being destroyed'.

Another story related by Mr Beaver is that of Henry Dean, a cousin of Lady Harrison. Apparently this unfortunate man was forced to earn his living as a publican after lending money to John Hawes, a brewer of Wokingham. The money was never repaid. As if this was not enough, Dean's involvement in the Civil War reduced his income still further until he had nothing left but a tenement of £3 a year. At 50 years of age he became a gardener, a hard life for a man 'not being used to work'. He followed this occupation until he was 80 years of age. It is a comfort to know that in spite of these misfortunes Henry Dean remained 'patient, healthy, and of a cheerful and honest heart'. He died at the age of 85. Obviously he had thrived on hard work but Benjamin Beaver added a warning note:

Let this deter others lest they ruin themselves and their families as Algernon, Alexander, and the said Richard did theirs

Lastly an epitaph which says much about the trials of an 18th century coachman in a very few words. It is inscribed upon the tomb of James Murray in Speen churchyard. Many coaches travelled through that village on their way from London to Bath and the coachman had no easy task to drive the heavy vehicles along the rutted roads in all weathers, to please their passengers, to be on the alert for possible attacks from highwaymen, and satisfy their employers and innkeepers by keeping to the scheduled timetables. It was a long hard road and for one the end of the journey appears to have been a welcome release from his trials and tribulations.

In memory of
James Murray
Late Bath Coachman
who died 20th May, 1796
Aged 46 years.
Tho' while on earth I did remain
I was reproach and scorn by men
But now am numbered with the saints
and saf'd of all my long complaints.

Thomas Holloway

PATENT medicines became increasingly popular during the second half of the 19th century when affluent Victorians cast aside their well tried natural remedies in favour of the fashionable new products which filled the shelves of the apothecaries' shops. In the most prominent positions one was sure to see those bearing the brand name of HOLLOWAY. The demand for Thomas Holloway's products did not entirely depend upon their efficacy but also upon their producer's ability to advertise them. Members of the public were left in no doubt at all that Holloway's ointment and pills were essential to their well-being.

Are you in agony? – A Well Spring of Hope for all.
HOLLOWAY'S OINTMENT.

To the very core and centre of all diseases which effect the surface of the body this remarkable preparation penetrates.

It disappears as if it were literally drawn down by some internal force and performs its healing errand, safely and without pain.

This advertisement appeared in the *Reading Mercury* during 1860. It claimed that this wonderful ointment cured

a variety of complaints 'whether in the skin, the flesh, the glands, or among the muscles'. It could be obtained from 'The Establishment of Professor Holloway of 224 The Strand (near Temple Bar) London, and from all respectable druggists and dealers in medicine throughout the civilised world'.

The ointment ranged in price from 1s.1½d. to 33s. a pot but, it was pointed out, there was a considerable saving by buying the larger sizes!

During 1860 there was an outbreak of diptheria in Reading. At once another advertisement appeared which advised the townspeople to take Holloway's pills as soon as symptoms of a sore throat appeared so that the dreaded illness might be checked in its early stages. A masterful stroke of propaganda which sent the frightened populace scurrying to buy the precious pills. It was by grasping every such opportunity to promote his sales that this enterprising man succeeded in building up his very profitable business.

Thomas Holloway was born on 22nd September 1800 at Plymouth Dock (now Devonport) where his father, a retired warrant officer, had opened a baker's shop. Later the family moved to The Turk's Head Inn at Penzance, and Thomas attended school locally and at nearby Camborne until he reached the age of 16. When his father died, his mother was left to provide for her numerous family, and with the help of both sons, Henry and Thomas, she ran a grocery and bakery business in the Market Place at Penzance. Thomas remained with her until he was 28 when he felt that it was time for him to seek better prospects in London. Soon after his arrival in the city he met Miss Jane Driver whom he eventually married. It was to prove an ideal match as his wife joined enthusiastically in her husband's ventures throughout their married life.

After various jobs, in 1836 Thomas Holloway became a merchant and foreign commercial agent, an undertaking which was to change his life. Among his clients was a native of Turin, Felix Albinolo, who had settled in London. This man prepared an ointment from a secret recipe which he called 'Albinolo's or the St Come et St Damien ointment'. With Thomas Holloway's assistance it was accepted for use at St Thomas's Hospital, a circumstance which set Mr Holloway thinking that here was an opportunity to use his own skills. He considered the possibility of preparing a harmless concoction to be known as 'Holloway's family ointment'. It was on sale by October 1837.

A year later an advertisement appeared in *Town* accompanied by a recommendation for the ointment from no less a person than Herbert Mayo, the senior surgeon of the Middlesex Hospital. Thomas Holloway was on the road to success, but there were pitfalls during the early years after he established his small warehouse in the Strand and added the sale of pills to that of his now lucrative ointment. The advertisements proved very expensive and debts threatened to overwhelm him as they had overwhelmed Felix Albinolo, but Thomas and Jane lived simply and worked hard. With his wife to help him in the preparation of his remedies Holloway, a man of good looks and persuasive charm, was free to travel both the town and country regions to sell his wares. He also visited the dock areas where he took care to interest both sailors and travellers in his products. He assured them that the pills and ointments would safeguard them from illness both during the voyage and throughout their period abroad. In this way his preparations and the belief in their success were carried to foreign lands. Undoubtedly, some curative properties were present to give satisfaction, otherwise his customers would not have repeated their orders as they did. At length the business prospered, creditors were paid in full and Thomas and Jane Holloway began to reap the benefits of their hard work. They became immensely rich.

His warehouse in the Strand was demolished in 1867 to make way for the new Law Courts and so alternative premises were obtained in Oxford Street. Here a hundred people were employed in addition to the numerous salesmen. The proprietors lived on the premises, but as careful investments and successful speculations increased his wealth, Thomas Holloway looked for a suitable house away from London. As a result of their searchings, he and Jane moved to Tittenhurst at Sunninghill in Berkshire. Sadly his wife did not live long to enjoy her new home for she died in 1875 at the age of 71. There were no children of the marriage and the broken hearted widower looked for ways of spending his now vast fortune.

Surprisingly, his offer to benefit his native town was not well received by its officials, and so Thomas Holloway then sought the advice of Lord Shaftesbury who suggested that a sanatorium for the mentally afflicted would prove of great benefit. This idea was readily adopted and the building of a hospital at Virginia Water was commenced at once. It provided accommodation for 240 patients and when completed in 1885 it was opened by the Prince and Princess of Wales, later King Edward VII and Queen Alexandra.

In the meantime Thomas Holloway had conceived the idea of also erecting a ladies' college in memory of his beloved wife. In his usual businesslike manner he lost no time in translating thoughts into deeds. He purchased 90 acres of land at Mount Lee, Egham Hill, on 8th May 1876. This site, on the Berkshire/Surrey borders was to form the Holloway College estate.

The architect who was entrusted with the design of the proposed college was William Crossland. The result was an awe inspiring building embellished with ornately designed scrolls, fruit, flowers and shells on every corner and pinnacle and over every door and window. It has to be seen for the amount of work involved in it to be fully appreciated. Local bricks were used and every stage was carefully watched by the benefactor. Although so near to his home he had a bungalow built in the grounds so that he could be at hand to see the main building grow into a massive structure of 1,000 rooms, with a beautifully decorated chapel, a spacious library, and an art gallery. This gallery now houses the valuable and famous art collection which Holloway bought as he travelled Europe in search of pictures for his college. Alas, he was not to see them hung upon its walls or to watch the first students enter its doors or enjoy their leisure in its spacious grounds; he died shortly before his great work was completed. He had spent over £400,000 on the land, buildings, furnishings and pictures and he left another £300,000 to complete and endow the college.

A statue of the founder and his wife was placed in one quadrangle and in the other, one of Queen Victoria who opened the college on 30th June 1886. The room in which she was entertained remains the same to this day.

The Royal Holloway College, University of London, remained a women's college for nearly 80 years. It was only in 1965 that male undergraduates were admitted. In 1983 the college agreed to merge with Bedford College, University of London, and new buildings were erected in the grounds at Egham. The new institution known as the Royal Holloway and Bedford New College has places for nearly 3,000 undergraduates in the Arts, Sciences, and Music.

Thomas Holloway died at his home in December 1883. When he died he was spending £50,000 a year on his advertisements. These had been translated into several languages and his pills and ointments had acquired a world wide reputation.

After ensuring the continued welfare of his hospital and college, and providing for his faithful employees, he left the residue of his fortune to his wife's sister, Miss Mary Ann Driver. He was buried in the churchyard of St Michael's Church, Sunninghill, where a memorial chapel was later erected to the design of William Crossland.

The simple message on his churchyard memorial 'He, being dead, yet speaketh' symbolizes the work of a remarkable man whose remedies for sick bodies not only provided the money for the treatment of sick minds, but also enabled numerous women to receive a university education at a time when their status in life made it difficult for them to obtain such recognition. A fulfilment indeed of Thomas Holloway's desire to further education through a memorial to his devoted wife and partner.

Three VCs
of Thatcham

THATCHAM can surely lay claim to a rare, if not unique record for a village community. The Victoria Cross has been awarded to three of her sons, the first in the Boer War, the second in World War I, and the third in World War II. Furthermore, the last two awards were made to two brothers. The village is justifiably proud of these men and those who served with them during times of extreme danger.

Private William House of the 2nd Battalion, Royal Berkshire Regiment, returned home from South Africa in July 1902. He had been severely wounded in action but, according to the report in the *Newbury Weekly News,* he was looking wonderfully well considering all he had been through on the battlefield. He was awarded the Distinguished Conduct Medal for his bravery and Thatcham people felt proud of the young man whom they had known since his birth in 1879. He was the eldest son of Mr and Mrs Thomas House of Park Lane, Thatcham.

The year following his homecoming local pride was intensified by the announcement that the award of the DCM had been replaced by that of the Victoria Cross. This highest award for gallantry was conferred upon Private House for his conspicuous bravery at Mosilikatse

Nek, South Africa in 1900.

The 2nd Battalion which had joined a force stationed at Pretoria under the command of Sir Ian Hamilton, was moving westwards along the southern slopes of the Magliesburg range. On the northern slopes another column was marching parallel to the 2nd Battalion. In between the Boers were putting up a fierce resistance. An attempt was made by Sir Ian to force through a mountain pass so that he could make contact with the northern column. This manoeuvre resulted in a lengthy battle in the course of which a Sgt Gibbs went forward to reconnoitre. He was shot and fell severely wounded. Without a moment's hesitation Private House ran forward in an attempt to bring him to safety. He reached the wounded man, lifted him, and managed to carry him a few yards when he, too, was hit and fell amidst intense fire. Although in great pain he called out that no one was to go to his aid as the danger was too great.

After the South African war, Private House continued his career in the Army and volunteered for service in India. He returned to England in November, 1911, and shortly afterwards was promoted to the rank of lance corporal. He was stationed at Shaft Barracks, Dover. His friends noticed that since his return from abroad he was unusually quiet and sometimes appeared to be depressed but they were quite unprepared for the terrible event which occurred at the end of February 1912. As the lance corporal was preparing to go on parade he shot himself. It was thought that the Indian climate, coupled with the effect of the two severe head wounds which he had incurred in South Africa, had affected his health and caused temporary insanity. It was indeed a tragic end to a brave man's life.

The second Victoria Cross was awarded posthumously

to Second Lieutenant Alexander Buller Turner, 3rd Battalion (attached 1st) Royal Berkshire Regiment. He was the son of Major Charles Turner and Mrs Turner of Thatcham House and grandson of Admiral Sir Alexander Buller, GCB.

Described in the *Newbury Weekly News* as a 'lover of life and the happiness it brought' this 22 year old officer saved the lives of many by his outstanding bravery.

The local paper gave the following account of the award of his VC. 'To most conspicuous bravery on September 28th 1915 at 'Fosse 8' near Vermelles. When the regimental bombers could make no headway in Slag Alley, second Lieutenant Turner volunteered to lead a new bombing attack.

He pressed down the communication trench practically alone, throwing bombs incessantly with such dash and determination that he drove the Germans back about 150 yards without a check. His action enabled the reserves to advance with very little loss and subsequently covered the flank of his regiment in its retirement thus probably averting the loss of some hundreds of men. This gallant officer has since died of wounds received in this action.'

In fact it was just three days after the battle, on 1st October that Lieutenant Turner died. He was buried at Cloques, France, and is commemorated by a wall plaque in Thatcham parish church.

The news of the award of the Victoria Cross was received with gratification by those who had served with the young lieutenant. They shared the opinion of one who said, 'A pluckier man I never saw. I am proud to have served under such an officer'.

When this gallant act took place Victor, Alexander's younger brother, was a 15 year old schoolboy at Winchester. He was commissioned into the army three years later and was to prove a valued officer.

In 1942 Lieutenant Colonel Victor Buller Turner was serving with the Rifle Brigade (Prince Consort's Own) in the Western Desert. On the night of 27th October he led the men of his battalion through 4,000 yards of difficult terrain to their objective. They successfully accomplished their mission and took 40 German prisoners. The Colonel then organised the captured position for all-round defence. They needed it. He and his men came under continual enemy fire from 5.30 am to 7 am as 90 German tanks advanced in waves upon their isolated position. Thirty five enemy tanks were destroyed and another 20 were immobilised. Wherever the fighting was heaviest Lieutenant Colonel Turner was there encouraging his men. When he found that one nine pounder gun was being manned by only one officer and a sergeant he stayed to act as loader and together the three men accounted for five enemy tanks being destroyed. Although wounded in the head Victor Buller Turner refused aid until the last tank was out of action. For his personal gallantry, fine leadership, and complete disregard of danger he was awarded the Victoria Cross, just 27 years after his elder brother had received the same honour.

The story of the third VC has a happier ending than those of the other two heroes. Lieutenant Colonel Victor Buller Turner lived to see the end of the Second World War. His father had died in 1926 but his mother still lived in Thatcham and he returned home to his native village. After her death he decided to leave Thatcham and live in Suffolk where he died at the age of 72. The Berkshire village will long remember its three courageous soldiers, and if you visit the area of the Turner home there, Thatcham House, you will find that the road around it commemorates the gallant name – Turner's Drive.

Cippenham's Royal Marriage

AS ONE stands on the bridge over the M4 motorway at Cippenham the past and the present are brought vividly together by the surrounding scene.

New housing estates and industrial buildings stand beyond the hedgerows. Below, a continuous stream of traffic divides the fields which once formed part of the medieval domain of Richard, Earl of Cornwall, second son of King John and brother to Henry III. Nearby the remains of an ancient moat is thought to mark the site where his castle stood in the midst of his deer park. It was to this castle that the young earl brought his bride, Isabella, in the spring of 1231.

It was in some respects a remarkable match. Richard was 22 years old. The bride was nine years his senior, the widow of Gilbert de Clere, Earl of Gloucester, to whom she had borne six children in their 16 years of marriage. Isabella had married de Clere when she was only 14 years of age, and was widowed when he died in Brittany in 1230 while campaigning with Henry III and Richard of Cornwall. The earl's body was taken to Tewkesbury Abbey for burial and the bereaved countess remained there under the protection of the Abbot.

Isabella de Clere was a renowned noblewoman. Not

only was she the widow of the Earl of Gloucester but she was also the third daughter of the late William the Marshall, Earl of Pembroke. Of all his ten children, five sons and five daughters, she was held to be the one who most resembled her father, having inherited in good measure his bravery, ability, and charm of manner. Even as a child William had proved himself, when his father, John Marshall, had sent him as a hostage to King Stephen during the siege of Newbury Castle in 1152. Twice John Marshall placed his son's life in jeopardy when he failed to comply with the agreed terms, thereby arousing the justifiable anger of the king who threatened the boy with death. On both occasions the boy's outstanding courage and personal charm stayed the king's hand. Not only did Stephen spare the child's life but he chose to amuse his young hostage. In turn they plucked the flowers from a plant, probably the common plantain, as they played the old game of Soldiers or Speargrass.

As William grew to manhood he was destined for high honours throughout his long life. A gallant soldier and wise statesman he served England well, and as a revered elder statesman, William the Marshall, Earl of Pembroke, lord of Striguil (Chepstow) and lord of Leinster, became Regent of England during the early years of Henry III's minority. The whole country mourned his passing when he died in 1219, in his 80th year, at his manor of Caversham, surrounded by his family, church dignitaries, and statesmen. The Earl was succeeded by his eldest son, another William, who married Eleanor, daughter of King John, and sister to Henry III and Richard, Earl of Cornwall. It was to William Marshall the younger, his brother-in-law, that Richard turned for permission to marry the beautiful Isabella.

The matter was one of urgency. King Henry had

spoken of finding a suitable bride for his younger brother, but Richard had no wish to marry a woman of his brother's choosing purely for political reasons. He had seen Isabella and had fallen deeply in love with her. The Earl was convinced that no other woman would make him happy. In the early part of 1231 he rode in haste to Striguil where William Marshall was staying and laid his proposal before him. William gladly gave his consent and promised to help. Both men knew that they would incur the King's displeasure when they decided to keep the marriage secret until it was safely accomplished rather than risk any interference from Henry.

Richard left Striguil to make his way to Tewkesbury where he found Isabella and soon persuaded her to accept his proposal. She then travelled to her brother's castle at Caversham and in due course the marriage party proceeded to Fawley, another Thames-side manor of the Earl Marshall. There the wedding took place on the 13th March 1231.

The young earl lost no time in taking his bride to his castle at Cippenham but it was not a great stronghold and they must have waited in some trepidation for news of the reaction of the King when he learned of the secret and hasty union of his brother and heir to the throne. No doubt the earl and his new countess were poised for flight and may well have been forced to seek a safer refuge than Cippenham's wooden castle but for the Countess of Pembroke, who acted as peacemaker between her two brothers.

At length the King accepted the defeat of his own plan for Richard's future and sent for the newly-wed pair to attend him at Windsor. They must have travelled to the fortress with some misgivings but they were well received by Henry and Isabella's beauty and ability soon found favour in the eyes of her royal brother-in-law.

One month after the marriage, on the 13th April, the King presided at a banquet which he gave in honour of the occasion and was particularly gracious and courteous to the bride. She had indeed inherited the good qualities of her father and once again the courage and charm of a Marshall succeeded in calming the anger of a king.

The Castle Inn
Scandal

THE meeting and dinner of the Colnbrook Turnpike Commissioners which was held at the Castle Inn, Salthill, on 29th March 1773 not only brought illness and death in its wake but also an aftermath of deception, misplaced loyalties, and false accusations, which all added furore to the mystery surrounding the tragic event.

At first the news of what was happening to the commissioners was sketchy as though the principals in the drama were loath to admit the seriousness of the affair, but as the days passed and the death-toll mounted the county and London newspapers took up the story of that fateful day.

The *Berkshire Chronicle* published a full report of the proceedings on the 26th April 1773. The names of the gentlemen who were present at the meeting were given as follows: Honourable Mr O'Brien, Mr Needham, Edward Mason, Major Mayne, – Cheshire, Walpole Eyre, Esq., Captain Salter, Mr Isherwood, Mr Benwell, treasurer, Mr Pote senior and Burcombe, the surveyor.

The dinner, which was described as 'plain and innocent', offered a surprisingly wide range of food, namely: turtle soup, fish, jack, perch and eel spitch-cocket, fowls, bacon and greens, veal cutlets, ragout of pigs' ears, chine of mutton and salad, course of lamb and cucumber, crayfish, pastry, and jellies.

Within a short time (and this period of time was not clearly defined), nearly all the gentlemen were taken ill and in the cases of Captain Needham, Mr Eyre, Mr Isherwood, Mr Benwell and Mr Burcombe the illness proved fatal. Major Mayne was still dangerously ill.

Naturally, the first suspicions were cast on the food and drink that had been consumed at the dinner, but the landlady of the Castle Inn, Mrs Partridge, opened her kitchen and cellar for inspection. It was stressed that nothing was highly seasoned, and nothing could give cause for suspicion or any bad consequences. The wine, madeira, and port were of a good quality, and the company had not eaten or drunk to excess. So it was considered that no blame could be attached to the meal. Rather, it was thought, the illness could be attributed to the condition of a pauper who was brought to the inn with other poor people for examination by the magistrates.

It was the custom of those days to return the poor to their own parishes if possible so that the liability for their upkeep should not fall upon a parish in which they had taken up temporary residence. As some of the commissioners were also Justices of the Peace it had seemed convenient to hold a meeting on the same morning as the Turnpike meeting to decide the fate of these poor souls. All the gentlemen remained in the room apart from Mr Pote, a printer from Eton, who had attended the commissioners on business but left the room to take a stroll in the garden during the magisterial meeting. He was the only one who was not taken ill although he later dined with the commissioners.

Dr James, who was attending the seriously ill Major Mayne, was of the opinion that his illness, and that of the deceased, had been caused by infection and not occasioned by anything they had eaten or drunk, as the first symptoms did not occur until eleven days after the meeting whereas an illness of a poisonous nature would have occurred within hours of taking the poison.

In support of this theory it was said that one of the deceased, Mr Burcombe, the surveyor, had not dined with the commissioners but had eaten beefsteaks below stairs. Regarding the wine, it was pointed out that the gentlemen drank of the same wine which they had commended at their former meetings, and which many had drunk before and since the occasion.

So it appeared that the blame was upon the distressed pauper or, and this was another possibility, upon some felons who were being transferred from Reading Gaol to London for transportation. It so happened that these poor wretches had stopped at the inn that morning and it was suggested that one of them could have been suffering from gaol fever. Rumours were rife and heated discussions took place as to the cause of the tragedy.

Mrs Partridge must have been relieved that these alternative suggestions countered speculation about the quality of the fare she offered to her customers but the matter was not to rest so easily. As the *Chronicle* reported on 7th May 1773, 'the late unhappy affair at Salt Hill has made a great noise through every part of the country'. It was to continue to do so for some time in spite of a letter which was sent to Mrs Partridge by Dr James and Dr Huck that they were in agreement that the disease was of a contagious nature.

This opinion was confirmed by a Dr Hugh Kennedy, who was called upon to attend Captain O'Brien. He asserted that he had had considerable experience in the treatment of gaol fever, both in this country and abroad, and he was convinced that his patient was suffering from a putrid disorder which he was treating with success. Dr Kennedy was also convinced that it was caught from the pauper who, he had been told, could not stand without support.

However, a 'Wellwisher to the Public', as a correspondent from Windsor styled himself, was not so sure the pauper was to blame. He asserted that reports published to the effect that the illness was caused by a contagious disease (and Mr Pote of Eton had circulated handbills in support of this theory) were extremely suspect. He accused the propagators of such theories of spreading them for their own interests and to the detriment of the town of Windsor.

In support of his accusations he added that a report that the symptoms did not appear till Good Friday, eleven days after the meeting 'is untrue for it is known that Mr Isherwood was given over before that time, and the whole company were taken ill the very night following the dinner which is a fact known to everyone, whatever Dr James, or somebody for him may assert. Again Mr Burcombe, the surveyor, who ate his beefsteak below, is no proof that the wine he drank above stairs did not affect him in the manner which has since brought him to the grave but, on the contrary, the strongest argument for it'.

'Wellwisher' also argued, with good reason, that if the pauper had passed on the disease to the commissioners, why had none of the servants below caught it, likewise the people where the poor wretches had lodged? He considered that Mrs Partridge should endeavour to trace the vagrants, especially the extremely distressed one, to confirm or deny these queries.

The anonymous correspondent had obviously made inquiries about the condition of the commissioners who had survived the ordeal. Captain O'Brien was still not quite out of danger. Captain Salter, who had been taken ill immediately upon returning home, had drunk warm salt water which had made him vomit. Mr Mason was then under a course of salt water drinking which produced the same effect. Mr Williams (who was not mentioned in the original list) went to Chichester directly after the dinner. He developed a high fever and called a physician who cared for him properly so that he recovered. Mr Cheshire had dosed himself with strong physic as soon as he felt unwell with apparent success. A final comment: 'How Mr Pote escaped is hard to account for unless the soup which he ate before dinner could fortify his stomach.'

The report continued, 'Had the disease been contagious all or some of those who attended the disease must have been affected but nothing like that had appeared, though Dr James perhaps insured their lives as he had endeavoured to insure the reputation of Mrs Partridge's house by injudiciously opposing his physical reasoning to known facts and all for what? For supporting an individual at the expense of the quiet of the country; by this means setting a mark upon Windsor as an affected place, deterring strangers and injuring the inhabitants, when at this time there was no more wholesome place in Europe.' After these scathing comments 'Wellwisher' came to the conclusion that the wine had been tainted as several of the company had noticed a remarkable taste. He blamed the refiners of the wine and added that Mrs Partridge was to be pitied but for the public good it would be better if the truth was told rather than a tale of contagion which only scared the public.

Mrs Partridge promptly replied that she had indeed traced the history of the distressed pauper. On 30th April she had sent a letter to the *Gazetteer* affirming that James

Jackson, a poor fellow, was found ill in the stables of a Mr March at Taplow. He was carried into the house and nursed by the wife of one Matthews. She was taken ill of a fever but had recovered, but her husband had caught it and since died. Mrs Partridge added that the Revd Mr Hamilton of Taplow, and a Mr Newberry, would confirm this story.

James Jackson was then brought by cart by the parish officer to the Castle Inn on the 29th March and the gentlemen had ordered his removal to Wooburn. The poor man was taken by cart to an outhouse at the Royal Oak. Within ten days, Mrs Partridge asserted, the woman who carried food to Jackson was seized of a fever and died and the barber who shaved him was dangerously ill. It seemed that the Castle Inn landlady was on the way to successfully proving her innocence in the affair, but not for long.

On 28th May the *Berkshire Chronicle* printed 'Further particulars relative to Salthill' which not only included more theories about possible additions of various agents, including arsenic, in the refining of wine but also replied to Mrs Partridge's account of James Jackson's activities. It was stated that the pauper was not suffering from any contagious disease but the effects of lack of food and clothing, that the woman who had cared for him at Taplow was very well, and that her husbnd who had died had been ill for nine years. None of the March family who had helped him in his distress had suffered from any ill effects. Furthermore, the woman who had carried food to him at Wooburn was very old and very ill before she came into contact with him, and there were no cases of infectious disease in the county.

A final shaft at Mrs Partridge was the observation that none of her servants, who were numerous, had caught the infection although they had come into contact with the pauper.

Having presented all known facts and correspondence regarding the case without solving the mystery, the press allowed the matter to rest. No doubt it was discussed for months around the county whenever people met together for business or pleasure. It says much for Mrs Partridge's reputation that many were ready to defend her and continued to use the Castle Inn. As in the past the Commisioners of the Colnbrook Turnpike Trust alternated the venue for their meetings between the Castle and Windmill Inns.

They might not have been so trusting had they but known the truth. It was finally revealed in the *Memoirs of Charlotte Papendick*, who was the assistant keeper of the wardrobe to Queen Charlotte and lived at Windsor. (*The Great Bath Road* by Daphne Phillips). Apparently Mrs Partridge confessed on her deathbed that the turtle soup was the cause of the disaster. It had been left overnight in a copper pan, the bottom of which had become green with verdigris. When the soup was reheated in the morning the existing poison had become aggravated by the addition of acid flavourings. For years Mrs Partridge had kept her awful secret, plagued, no doubt, by her conscience which finally made her confess her guilt. To her credit she stated that the cook was unaware of the danger and was in no way to blame for the accident.

It came to light also that Mr Burcombe, the surveyor, had not eaten beefsteak below stairs as had been originally claimed, but had dined from the remains of the upstairs meal. That accounted for his unfortunate demise but what of Mr Pote's miraculous escape from harm?

Could the clue to his good fortune be in 'Wellwisher's' comments, 'unless the soup which he ate before dinner could fortify his stomach'? Obviously, this soup could not have been of the turtle variety which was served to the gentlemen. Perhaps another had been prepared for general consumption and, after his stroll in the garden, Mr Pote had taken a bowl of this variety *before* dinner as stated by 'Wellwisher', with the result that he refused the turtle soup when he sat down to dine. If this supposition is correct it could explain why Mr Pote alone suffered no sickness amongst those who dined at the Castle Inn on that ill-fated March day in 1773.

The Newbury Coat

JOHN COXETER of Greenham soon realized the advantages of the new machinery which was being installed in the mills of Britain during the early 19th century and he was determined to bring his own cloth mill up to date. So proud was he of his modernised premises that he boasted he could take a coat from a man's back, reduce it to wool, and remake the coat in the space of 24 hours.

Sir John Throckmorton of Buckland, hearing the boast, asked if it would be possible to make a coat by sunset from wool which had been growing on a sheep's back at sunrise. This proposition needed thought for Sir John was willing to place a wager of 1,000 guineas if Mr Coxeter thought the feat possible.

After every detail had been considered Sir John was told to place his wager and plans were set afoot for the making of the coat between 5 am and 8 pm on a summer's day.

On the morning of Tuesday, 25th June 1811, Sir John's shepherd Francis Druett, brought two Southdown sheep to Greenham mill. Three stewards stood by to see fair play and as the sun rose the order was given to start shearing. The wool fell under the shepherd's expert hands and was quickly gathered and taken into the mill where it was washed, stubbed, and roved before being handed to the spinners. The young women worked swiftly at their wheels and soon the first spools were with John Coxeter, junior, who was waiting at his loom. Not by virtue of his relationship had he been chosen – time was too precious for such favours. A competition had been held and he had proved himself to be the fastest weaver in his father's mill.

By four pm the cloth had been scoured, fulled, tented, raised, sheared, dyed, and dressed, and placed into the hands of the tailor, Mr Isaac White of Newbury, who had already measured Sir John.

The cloth was deftly cut by the tailor's son, James, as nine men waited with needles threaded. Gradually the garment took shape, a hunting coat of fine kersey dyed to the fashionable shade of Wellington, a rich damson colour. It was double breasted with turned up cuffs and long tails after the fashion of the day.

By twenty minutes past six, an hour and forty minutes before the allotted time, the coat was finished and presented to Sir John who proudly exhibited it to the 5,000 people who had gathered before the mill. That evening, resplendent in his new coat, he sat down to dine in the company of 40 friends at Newbury's famous Pelican Inn – the inn which by its prices inspired an earlier guest to write the following verse:

> The famous inn at Speenhamland
> That stands below the hill
> May well be called the Pelican
> From its enormous bill.

On the night of 25th June 1811 all was satisfied contentment and the proprietor, Mr George Botham received no complaints.

The two sheep had been killed and roasted, a sad end for the suppliers of the fine wool. However, the crowd enjoyed an unexpected supper, especially as it was washed down by 120 gallons of beer, thoughtfully provided by the jubilant Mr Coxeter.

In 1851 the coat was shown at the Great Exhibition. An oil painting of the event by Luke Clint stood beside it so that all could see the story of its origin. John Coxeter received a silver medal from the Berkshire Agricultural Society.

Although the Buckland Estate has now been sold by the Throckmortons the coat is safely housed at the family seat, Coughton Court, near Alcester, where it is justly known as the Throckmorton Coat.

In September 1991, a bid was made at the Newbury Agricultural Show to beat the record set for making the original Newbury coat. This succeeded, with the second Newbury coat being completed in just 12 hours 36 minutes and 26 seconds.

Mary Russell Mitford

THE cottage in Three Mile Cross where Mary Russell Mitford lived for 30 years has been converted into offices, and the tree lined turnpike road between Reading and Basingstoke now vibrates to the roar of 20th century traffic, but beyond the village lie the fields, the woods, and the lanes where Miss Mitford once walked with Mayflower, her beloved greyhound. Occasionally she would stop to exchange greetings with her friends. There was shy Hannah, destined to marry the son of a wealthy hatter of Reading, the industrious, pale, and sickly looking shoemaker, Joe Kirby the young cricketer, and Lizzie, the seven year old daughter of the village carpenter. All these, and many more, she introduced into the pages of her famous book *Our Village*.

The authoress was not a native of Berkshire. She was born in Alresford, Hampshire, on 16th December 1787, the only surviving child of Dr George Mitford and his wife, Mary. The doctor was not a busy country practitioner as one might suppose, but a gentleman of leisure. He had married an heiress, ten years his senior, and was quite content to live on her income and indulge his passion for gambling. Fortune did not always smile upon him. During Mary's childhood the family moved to Reading,

Lyme Regis, and finally to London, by which time his wife's fortune was so depleted that George Mitford was in serious financial difficulties, but he still retained the gambler's optimistic hope that his luck must change.

When Mary's tenth birthday was at hand the doctor took the child to purchase her present – a lottery ticket! She was allowed to choose the number and immediately selected 2224. The lottery office keeper shook his head. Part of that ticket was already sold. Mary was told to choose another number but she was adamant. It must be 2224 as the total of those numbers represented her age. The keeper probably thought her a precocious and troublesome child, but her father regarded her insistence as a propitious omen. He bought out the part owner of the ticket and Mary had her present. For once, Dr Mitford's intuition did not fail him. Ticket number 2224 won a prize of £20,000.

Having disposed of his wife's money George Mitford now lost no time in spending that of his daughter. He purchased a house in London Road, Reading. Here he became friendly with M. St Quintin, a French refugee, whose wife taught at the Abbey School. Later the St Quintins opened a school in London at 22 Hans Place where Mary was sent as a boarder in 1798. It was probably the best thing that Dr Mitford ever did for her. By 18th century standards she received a good education and returned home in 1802 an accomplished young lady with a taste for literature.

Mary Mitford's first published work *Miscellaneous Poems* appeared in 1810 and further volumes of poetry found favour both in this country and in America. She visited London frequently, moved in literary circles, and made influential friends. These included Samuel Coleridge who encouraged her to write tragic poetical works.

It was providential that she was so talented. By 1820 her father had once more reduced his family to penury after buying and lavishly rebuilding a farmhouse in Grazely where he, his wife, and daughter enjoyed an elegant lifestyle until mounting debts forced them to leave their home. They found refuge in a labourer's cottage which was situated between the village inn and a general shop in Three Mile Cross. After the spaciousness of Bertram House, their Grazely home, the cramped conditions of the cottage must have been almost unbearable. The largest room was eight feet square. With her customary resilience to misfortune Mary proceeded to plant the garden with her favourite flowers in an endeavour to brighten the mean surroundings of her new home.

Now her writing was the only means of support for the family. Apparently it did not occur to Dr Mitford that he should exert himself to improve his income. In her own words, Mary Russell Mitford descended 'from the lofty steep of tragic poetry to the every day path of village stories'. It was to prove a path paved with success.

The first sketches of village life appeared in the *Lady's Magazine* in 1819. The sales of the periodical rose sharply as readers clamoured for more news from 'Our Village'. They eagerly awaited the stories of the village cricket matches, the day to day events in the lives of the villagers, the descriptions of the wild creatures and the hedgerow flowers so vividly portrayed by the authoress.

Early stories were published in one volume in 1824. It was the first of many, so popular have the tales remained to this day.

Not that poetry and plays were altogether neglected. Mary Mitford also enjoyed success as a playwright. *Julian* (1823) and *Foscari* (1826) were both produced at Covent Garden and *Rienzi* (1828) at Drury Lane Theatre. This play, a poetical tragedy was considered her best work for the theatre. It ran for 34 performances and 8,000 copies were sold.

In November 1829 *Foscari* and *Rienzi* were produced by Edward Barnett at Reading Theatre. In both plays the lead was taken by Mr Cathcart whose acting ability was held in high esteem by Miss Mitford. She attended the theatre regularly to write reviews of Mr Barnett's presentations for the *Reading Mercury*.

Mary's mother died in 1830 leaving Mary to provide and care for her wayward father. A thankless task indeed. Not only did he squander his daughter's money but he made demands upon her time by asking her to read aloud to him and to bear him company. He hated to be alone and resented her absence if she visited her friends. In spite of all hindrances the plays, poems, reviews, and contributions to various magazines, flowed from her pen. Another major work *Belford Regis*, or *Sketches of a Country Town* appeared in 1835 and her Berkshire readers had no difficulty in recognizing Reading as the subject of this book. It enjoyed considerable success although it lacked the spontaneous charm of *Our Village*. Elizabeth Barrett (afterwards Mrs Browning) thought well of it and was able to convey her personal congratulations to the authoress when the two ladies were introduced to each other in 1836 on one of Miss Mitford's now rare visits to London. They became firm friends and corresponded frequently. The grant of a civil pension of £100 a year made in 1837 helped alleviate financial pressure, at least for a time, and later that year alterations were made to the cottage at Three Mile Cross. Miss Mitford wrote to tell her new friend about 'a pretty upstairs sitting room, 13 ft square, with a little ante-room lined with books, both looking on to the garden'. At last she could write in comparative comfort.

Unfortunately, her financial troubles were by no means at an end. Early in 1842 Mary admitted that she had not bought a gown, cloak, bonnet, or hardly a pair of new gloves for four years, but she never once criticized or blamed her spendthrift father. He died later that year, on 11th December, and left a pile of debts to be settled by his long-suffering daughter. The bills were paid by public subscription and the surplus that remained helped to boost Mary's scanty savings.

Her health began to deteriorate but her spirit remained undaunted. Her great friend, the Revd Charles Kingsley, rode over from his parish of Eversley to see her, and other friends travelled from London to the little cottage where she continued to live until 1851. Then she decided to move nearer to her friend Lady Russell of Swallowfield Park.

It is said that Mary Mitford's beloved books were packed on a hand cart and pushed along the lanes to her new home. This story was verified a few years ago by an old lady who recalled that her grandfather had seen the occurrence when he was a boy in Swallowfield. Unfortunately, shortly after her move a carriage accident while she was being driven through Swallowfield Park caused severe injuries and she became confined to the house.

In 1852 *Recollections of a Literary Life* was published, and two years later, *Atherton and other Tales*. This book was highly praised by John Ruskin and it was to be her last. Mary Russell Mitford died on 10th January 1855. By her own request she was buried in Swallowfield Churchyard and not, as her friends had expected, at Shinfield Church where her parents were buried, near the village of Three Mile Cross.

Perhaps she chose wisely. The quiet corner where a granite cross marks her resting place remains unchanged. The nearby footpath still leads across Swallowfield Park, and the great house, now divided into elegant flats, retains the grandeur of more gracious days when Lady Russell sent her carriage to fetch Miss Mitford for afternoon tea.

A Lambourn
Celebration

'ONE of the wildest and most neglected in the diocese of Oxford'. So Frances Milman described the parish of Lambourn in her biography of her brother Robert when he became vicar in 1851. Nothing daunted, he set about reforming his errant parishioners and despite acting the role of policeman as well as parson, over the eleven years of his office he came to earn the love and respect of the villagers. His reforms included the building, largely at his own expense, of a new church at nearby Eastbury, with a school and master's house, and the restoration of the chancel of Lambourn church.

Despite his skilled horsemanship and care for parishioners who worked in racing stables he strongly disapproved of horse racing – in a village devoted to horses. It was this clash of views that led villagers to take drastic action against his authority.

In her biography Frances Milman does not give a date for the incident, but it has been linked to Kettledrum, the horse that brought honour to Lambourn in 1861, the year before the Reverend Milman left the parish to continue his pastoral work in India.

Kettledrum, a chestnut colt, was sent from Lancashire to Lambourn to complete his training by his owner,

Colonel Townsend, who had high hopes for his horse after it had come second to Diophantus in the 2,000 Guineas while still partly trained. Accompanied by his trainer, George Oates, Kettledrum was taken to Prince's stables near Lambourn to be prepared for the 1861 Derby.

The race was marred by a controversial start and an ill-conditioned course. Kettledrum, ridden by a young jockey called Bullock, was up against the favourite, Dundee, who stumbled just before reaching the winning post, allowing Kettledrum to overtake him and win the Derby. Dundee's legs had caused some concern before the race; afterwards it was discovered that one foreleg was almost broken. In spite of this the gallant horse finished second to Kettledrum, whose owner admitted that but for his injury Dundee would have been the winner.

However, these considerations did not detract from the feeling of exultation that pervaded the Lambourn racing fraternity. Kettledrum had won – that was all that mattered to the parishioners of Lambourn on the night of 29th May 1861. Elated by his success, they asked the Reverend Milman for permission to ring the church bells in celebration of the victory. Not surpisingly, in view of his disapproval of horse racing, the vicar refused. The villagers were not to be thwarted; they broke into the church, barricaded themselves in the tower, and rang a peal in honour of the occasion. Furious, the vicar summoned the ringers before the magistrates – there are no records as to their fate, but on the following Sunday the congregation was left in no doubt as to the Reverend Robert Milman's feelings. The strength with which he expressed these, so intimidated his parishioners that for the remainder of his ministry no one dared to ignore his strictures on the abuse of the Church for the celebration of the Turf.

King James
and the Tinker

TWO counties claim the story of the King and the tinker. I heard the legend as a child growing up in the Middlesex town of Enfield where King James I enjoyed hunting in Enfield Chase, and it is claimed that there he met the tinker, outside the old inn which proudly bears the name, The King and Tinker. Traditionally the site of one of the oldest taverns in the country, it is situated near Theobalds Park where the King was often entertained by Robert Cecil. The King's preference for Theobalds over his own residence, the Old Palace at Hatfield resulted in the exchange of the two properties. The Cecils began their long association with Hatfield and the King enjoyed his hunting lodge at Theobalds.

Some years ago I found the story of the King and the tinker in the *Book of Berkshire Ballads* edited by the late Mr John Brain, but here the scene of the legend is close to Windsor, at Braywood Side. The inn of the story was known as The Royal Black Bridge, and New Lodge, near the site of the Royal Kennels, the presumed place where the tinker was knighted – but let us feel as carefree as King James on that sunny morning and dwell not on where the meeting occured, joining the King 'as he was a-chasing his fair fallow deer'.

Through the forest he rode until, tired of his courtiers and the hunt, he slipped away in search of new pleasures and spurred his horse along the lane where he came upon a lonely ale-house. On a wooden bench outside sat a tinker, his jug before him, but let the ballad take up the tale:

'Honest fellow what has thou in thy jug?'
inquired the King.
'In truth', said the tinker, 'tis nappy brown ale
And to drink unto thee, good faith, I'll not fail,
What though thy jacket looks gallant and fine,
I hope that my twopence as good is as thine.'

The King laughingly accepted the tinker's plea for equality and they fell into easy conversation as they called for their pitchers of ale and sat together outside the inn. The King inquired if the mender of kettles had gathered any news on his travels, but the tinker replied that the only tale in which he was interested was the rumour that the King was hunting in the forest and might pass by the inn. In all his journeys through the land he had never seen good King James and it would bring him much happiness if he could do so that very day.

The monarch was pleased with such honest and simple loyalty, and suggested that if the tinker could ride behind him they might go together to seek the King. The tinker leapt to his feet with excitement but as he stopped to gather up his belongings a thought struck him; what if the huntsmen were dressed so finely that he could not recognise the King as the cavalcade passed by in pursuit of the deer? The King had a ready reply:

'I tell thee, good fellow, when thou dost come there,
  The King will be covered, the Nobles be bare'.

Satisfied, the tinker hesitated no longer but quickly
picked up his sack, his purse, and the tools of his trade,
and clambered up behind the King.

At length the new found friends reached a clearing in
the greenwood where the bareheaded nobles stood
anxiously awaiting the return of their errant monarch.
They sighed with relief as he rode into their midst, but
their puzzled eyes were upon the King's strange
companion. He, in turn, gazed upon them, and he was
very disappointed. All were finely dressed, all were bareheaded. Where was the King?

The tinker turned to his companion for an explanation
and received a shattering reply. As they were the only two
men wearing their hats, it must be one of them.

The poor man fell to the ground and begged mercy for
his stupidity. The King's request for his name did nothing
to soothe his fear. It was with difficulty that he stammered
' 'Tis John of the Vale'. The King drew his sword but
instead of the sharp blow which the tinker expected he felt
a light tap on his shoulder, 'Rise up, Sir John, and I will
make you a knight of five hundred a year'.

As if that were not enough excitement for one day the
old ballad tells us that the newly created knight attended
the Court that very evening

'where fresh store of pleasure and pastimes were seen
  In the royal presence of both King and Queen.'

When the tinker eventually sought his bed that night it
seems extremely doubtful if even he knew whether he was
in Enfield or Windsor.

Tales
of the
Bath Road

THE highway from London to Bath has seen changes in its fortunes and in its travellers as one mode of travel has superseded another, but it has always managed to survive to remain one of the most widely used roads in the kingdom.

Its heyday was undoubtedly in the great coaching days when its inns were famous for their hospitality and good stables. From the sporting buck in his light curricle to the coachman driving the heavy stage coach, the customers were sure of good food and a swift change of horses along the road. The section which passes through Berkshire was well served by hostelries.

The landlords thought themselves secure in the prosperity of the age as the gentry travelled to Bath to seek the cure of the medicinal springs after an exhausting London season. But change can strike swiftly and it was with despair that those same landlords saw the opening of the new-fangled railroad in 1838. At first it ran only to Slough but by 1841 it was opened to Bath and Bristol – the heyday of the road had passed.

It is true that market days brought custom as the

farmers, the carriers, and the drovers travelled to the nearest market town, but they returned home at nightfall, and the once busy stable yards no longer resounded with the stamping of impatient hooves and the jingling of harnesses as the horses were changed for the next stage of the journey.

But the railways in their turn fell on hard times as the 'horseless carriage' made its appearance. Only a few of these contraptions travelled the road at first but the tide had turned, and once again the Bath Road had come into its own. The stable yards were converted into the all important car parks!

The popularity of the motor car increased; coaches and lorries joined the merry throng, and the old highway was hard pressed to cope with all the traffic. The Bath Road became the motorists' nightmare as long queues formed and accidents were all too frequent. Another road must be made, they cried, and so the M4 motorway was opened and the residents who lived along Bath Road sighed with relief as they revelled in the uncanny quietness of a nearly deserted road. Not for long; gradually the traffic has built up again as many prefer to take the more leisurely road through town and village. As travellers relax in the comfort of an old established hotel, and delight in the atmosphere created by sporting prints, horse brasses, and hunting horns, they drain their glasses and tell the tales of the old Bath Road.

Long ago, another traveller rode into the courtyard of The Bear Inn at Maidenhead. It was King James I who once again had lost his hunting companions, and was tired and hungry after a day in the saddle. He called the landlord and inquired what he could offer in the way of refreshment. The worthy man, not recognising the King, said 'Nothing, Sir, it is Lent and all the fish is bespoke'.

He explained that the Vicar of Bray and his curate were dining at the inn and the available fish was being prepared for them. The King asked if he might join them, and having received the assent of the vicar, the landlord conducted the newcomer to the dining table.

All went well until the end of the meal when the King was forced to admit that he had no money on his person and could not pay his due. The vicar was displeased and did not hesitate to say so, but the curate begged to pay the stranger's reckoning, saying that he would think himself well repaid by his guest's entertaining conversation.

While the stranger was thanking the curate, the gentlemen of the hunt came to the inn inquiring if their master had been seen. King James stepped out, showing himself on the balcony, and the huntsmen in the courtyard below paid him homage, much to the discomfort of the vicar. However, the King must have been put into a good humour by his dinner, for he readily forgave the embarrassed cleric, saying that he should still remain the Vicar of Bray. He repaid the curate for his generosity by appointing him to a vacant Canonry of Windsor.

King James' son also came on a journey to Maidenhead but on a less happy occasion. It was to The Greyhound Inn, one of the most famous of the town's hostelries, that King Charles I was brought from his Roundhead prison at Caversham House to meet three of his children, James, Duke of York, and the two princesses. They were in the custody of the Earl of Northumberland, and were brought along the Bath Road from Syon House to meet their father.

So moved were the Roundheads who saw the royal reunion that permission was given for the children to return with their father to Caversham for the space of two days.

The Greyhound Inn was burnt to the ground in 1736; 'out of the thirty-six Standing Beds, only three feather beds and one pewter dish was saved; even all the Plate, Money, and Books were lost'. One of the 'best furnished inns in England' was no more.

A loss indeed to this town of many inns. These hostelries were made necessary by the large number of travellers who preferred to stay in the town overnight instead of driving through the dreaded Maidenhead Thicket at dusk, although it was said that the highwaymen who lurked under the trees preferred the coaches entering the town from the West of England. Those approaching from the London side had already been robbed by the highwaymen of Hounslow Heath.

Many tales are told of the highwaymen who frequented this famous road. Several were captured and after they were hanged at Tyburn their bodies were brought to suspend in chains from gibbets erected by the roadside, to serve as a warning to those who contemplated taking to the road for a living. In 1804 King George III was so nauseated by the sight of the dangling highwaymen that he ordered the bodies to be removed before he travelled from London to Windsor. In spite of such warnings and harsh penalties, men persisted in highway robbery, often in desperation as poverty, or even gambling debts, overtook their lives.

That much travelled gentleman of the road, Dick Turpin, would ride to Sonning where an aunt was ready to give him shelter and, if necessary, help him escape over the bridge into Oxfordshire. The faithful Black Bess found her own way to the hidden stable, there to wait for her master until the hue and cry had passed.

The most dashing of highwaymen, Claude Duval, owned a house at Wokingham. The 17th century Frenchman was noted for his gallantry, and is said to have danced with one fair lady by the roadside, after politely obtaining her husband's permission to do so. He gallantly returned her to her coach and graciously accepted only a light purse from her partner before riding off with his companions. For all his audacity, he reached the gallows in 1670 at the age of 27.

One who was not so well known perhaps, but seemed equally dangerous as the two more famous robbers, was Captain Hawkes. Slough was the principal area in which he worked but he had no objection to riding further afield.

He managed to evade capture for a number of years for he was a past master in disguise. He scorned the traditional mask and would appear as a Quaker, a country squire, a soldier or a parson, and demand money from his unsuspecting victims.

It was while he was dining frugally, as befitted his disguise as a Quaker, that a swaggering traveller entered the doors of the Plough Inn at Salt Hill. The newcomer bestowed a cursory glance upon the plainly clad man and threw his pistols down on the table.

The traveller ordered his own refreshment and proceeded to check his valuables. He remarked to the Quaker that by carrying firearms he had no need to fear the likes of Captain Hawkes, and advised the seemingly peace loving man to forget his scruples and to arm himself. The traveller gathered up his belongings and paid his bill. He did not notice the Quaker quietly leaving the inn.

Proceeding along the road, the confident man was suddenly alerted by the dreaded cry. 'Your money, or your life'. He was ready with his pistols but, alas for him, they did not fire. He faced the highwayman unarmed – and saw the Quaker!

Collecting the valuables which had been so carelessly

displayed, the highwayman advised the traveller to watch his pistols more carefully in future, and to refrain from boasting in front of strangers. With that good advice he rode off laughing, and that evening he came to the Rising Sun Inn at Woolhampton. There he sat enjoying a good supper after a hard day's ride.

Two country yokels shared his table, drinking their ale, but they soon began to quarrel and when one drew a knife, Captain Hawkes jumped up to intervene. It was his undoing. His arms were caught behind him by the strong arm of a Bow Street Runner. All too late the highwayman saw their red waistcoats under the yokels' smocks. Another notorious robber was removed from the road – and by men equally adept at disguise!

Others besides the professional 'gentlemen of the road' tried their hand at highway robbery.

There is a report in *The Reading Mercury* dated 2nd May 1835, stating that a robbery had taken place in Woolhampton the previous evening when Mr William and Mr Charles Hazell of Midgham were returning home from Reading in a one horse chaise. Near the Rising Sun they were suddenly assailed by four men, one of whom seized the horse's head, while the other three commenced their attack upon the gentlemen in the gig.

Whilst Mr Charles Hazell was endeavouring to beat off one of the villains with his whip, another presented a pistol at his brother's head, and a third got up behind the gig and secured Mr C. Hazell's arms, and in this position they were robbed of between £14-£15. After the villains had secured their booty they decamped across the fields without offering further violence.

A reward of £10 was offered for the rogues' apprehension, £5 from the unfortunate brothers, and £5 by the Bucklebury Association for the Protection of Property and

Prosecution of Felons. Whether the Woolhampton robbers were caught we do not know. A clue given in the reward advertisement said that one of them was wearing a very white smock-frock, so that he evidently had a good wife or mother to care for his appearance in spite of his addiction to crime.

Another 'hold-up' in a lighter vein was a festival that used to take place at Salt Hill when the boys of Eton College went to the Mount to gather 'salt' as it was called, but in reality money, which was donated towards the maintenance of a scholar at Cambridge. How much was left after the payment of the expenses of the day, which included the provision of fancy costumes and a banquet at night, is open to question, but as much as £1,000 could be collected on a good day.

Held annually in the years following its introduction in 1561, it developed into a triennial festival after 1775 and was discontinued in the mid-19th century after the excesses of the carnival spirit became too grave.

Kings and queens attended the ceremony and watched the boys collecting money from the passers-by, often holding up the coaches and exacting their dues from the travellers. Indeed, royalty contributed generously; George IV and Queen Charlotte, his mother, regularly gave 50 guineas each to the cause.

Queen Victoria and her consort were reluctant to see the end of the old custom but eventually agreed that it must cease if the good name of the college was not to be endangered.

The final story of the Bath Road begins over the county border in Wiltshire. The second Duke of Chandos, travelling along the road back to his home at Shaw House, Newbury, had stopped at Marlborough overnight. He was preparing to continue his journey the next morning when he heard the pitiful screams of a young girl.

Hurrying to investigate he saw an ostler savagely beating her. When the Duke intervened the man said that he had every right to treat her so, for she was his wife. However, seeing that His Grace was deeply concerned he offered to sell his wife to her wealthy protector for the sum of £20. His offer was accepted and the weeping girl was put into the ducal coach.

It transpired that she was the daughter of a Newbury man, John Wells, but she was sent to Stanmore and safely placed in the care of the vicar and his wife.

The Duke of Chandos was a married man, but later his wife died, and the ostler also being dead, he married his protégée in 1744. In spite of her humble origin his bride became a most gracious and beloved Duchess.

The Duke's connections with Shaw House were severed in 1751 when his mother died and he sold the historic Elizabethan house which had played so great a part in the Civil War, before King Charles made his sad journey to Maidenhead.

Hocktide
at Hungerford

THE town of Hungerford is steeped in history. The name itself goes back to legendary days and traditionally is derived from 'Hingward's ford', after a chieftain who was drowned while crossing the marshland where the waters of the Kennet now flow.

In 1540 King Henry VIII settled the Bear Inn on Anne of Cleves as part of her dowry, and later transferred his gift to Catherine Howard. Queen Elizabeth I slept at the inn on one of her many journeys round her kingdom, and it was here that William, Prince of Orange, met the King's Commissioners on 6 December 1688, just before King James II fled from the country, leaving his son-in-law as king.

John of Gaunt, Duke of Lancaster, was the chief benefactor of the town, for he presented its charter in 1360. He also presented a horn so that the Commoners could be called together to hear the proclamations of the day. A horn believed to be John of Gaunt's is preserved by the Manor, but its great age precludes its use at the ceremonies of today. By the Charter, 99 Commoners of Hungerford were originally granted Common rights, and rights of fishing in the River Kennet.

The privilege of using the river is indeed valuable for

it is a 'fayre river which yieldeth store of fishes and especiallie troutes' and the rights are jealously guarded. Crayfish are another delicacy as an old rhyme tells:

Hungerford crayfish, catch me if you can,
There's no such creature in the o-ce-an.

When the reigning monarch passes through Hungerford a red rose of Lancaster is presented with due ceremony to commemorate the granting of the Charter.

Old and picturesque customs pass away all too frequently, but Hungerford is a town which prides itself upon retaining its ancient ceremonies, particularly that of Hocktide.

On the first Tuesday after Easter week, the Hocktide Court is summoned. At eight o'clock in the morning the town crier steps on to the balcony of the Town Hall and sounds the horn which was presented to the town in 1634 by Jehosophat Lucas, Constable.

The crier then proceeds in turn to the High Street, Church Street, and Bridge Street, to repeat the summons. Any commoner who is unable to attend the Court is traditionally fined one penny, but I understand that coins of greater value are accepted by the crier to be distributed later to the children of the town.

The crier doubles his role with that of the assistant town bailiff. The office is held at the present time by Edwin Sidney (Robin) Tubb who became town crier in 1957 at the early age of 19. He is the fourth generation of his family to hold the office. His great-grandfather, Edward Bushnell was crier from 1880 to 1923. He was succeeded by his son Sidney Bushnell. Unfortunately, ill health forced Sidney to retire in 1957 but not before the Hocktide Ceremony had taken place that year. Sidney's niece, Mrs

Tubb (Robin's mother), then carried out the supplementary duties of the crier, but she was never called upon to try her vocal skills. Later in the year Robin Tubb was appointed as official crier, in good time to prepare for the 1958 Hocktide Court.

Having summoned the Court, the crier returns to the Town Hall to be present at the opening ceremony when the Commoners' Roll is called. When the name of an absentee is announced the crier steps forward and places one penny (from his collection of Victorian pennies) on the table, saying to the constable 'Here, Sir'.

The Hocktide Court then elects the constable for the ensuing year, together with the portreeve (mayor or principal magistrate), bailiffs, overseer of the common, tutti or tithing men, and ale tasters. These are the officers who, throughout the centuries, have ensured that law and order have been maintained in this riverside town, that fishing and grazing rights have not been abused, and that the ale has been brewed to the required standards. Before he can be appointed constable a man must first serve in the offices of tuttiman, bailiff, and portreeve.

Having been elected, the tuttimen are handed their staffs of office, poles beautifully decorated with flowers and orange and blue ribbons, a task undertaken by Robin's mother for several years. Now his daughter-in-law prepares the staffs, thus involving another generation of the family in this ancient ceremony. The tuttimen set out to visit those houses whose owners enjoy the common rights and collect the 'headpennies', a custom which dates from the time when two tithing men were appointed annually to keep the peace and watch over the behaviour of those in their tithing, for which they were entitled to collect a penny a head. They claim their privilege of a kiss from the lady of the house to whom they present an orange from the bag of the orangeman who accompanies them.

After the Hocktide Court has dealt with the business of town and manor, a luncheon is served where a toast 'To the immortal memory of John of Gaunt' is drunk in 'Ye ancient Plantagenet punch', the ingredients of which are a closely guarded secret.

Newcomers to the lunch are shod by having nails driven into the soles of their shoes, and money is thrown to the schoolchildren. At one time hot pennies were thrown, a rather unkind custom which was observed at many such festivals. If greedy children rushed forward to grab the pennies their fingers were often burned. At Hungerford nowadays the coins are mostly cold, but if any are heated to preserve an old tradition, the children are warned not to touch them until they have cooled down.

On the Sunday following the court, the constable and all the other officers attend the parish church with appropriate ceremony

Over the years many of the attendant festivities have been dropped, but a banquet and dances are held during Hocktide Week, and it is to be hoped that the old customs will be long continued in this delightful historic town with its wide street, bow fronted shops, and old coaching inns, still calling all who enjoy the peace of a small town, the river, and the open common.

Twyford and the Polehampton Charity

THE name of Edward Polehampton has been a household word in Twyford for over 270 years; ever since the foundations of three red brick buildings were laid opposite the Rose and Crown Inn. How local interest must have been caught as the buildings grew into a school, chapel, and master's house, and it was learned that it was a charitable foundation to benefit poor boys of the village.

Why did Mr Polehampton choose Twyford as the place for this generous gift? He never lived there, and appears to have no connection at all with this village, once situated on the main Bath to London road until a bypass released it from the continual roar of traffic.

To this day the riddle has never been clearly solved but two tales are told, each giving a reason for his munificence.

One story relates that he was passing along the road to London with his young wife when she became ill. The landlord of the inn was kind to the invalid and her worried husband and, in gratitude for his hospitality, the village was remembered by Edward Polehampton when he was disposing of his wealth.

The second story, which is the most favoured, certainly

115

provides good reason for the benefactor's concern for poor boys. It tells that he came to the village as a little lad, destitute and alone, and sank in despair on the doorstep of the Rose and Crown Inn. It was Christmas Eve in the year 1666. The landlord went to the door and found the pathetic child. Was his heart stirred by thoughts of another Child who found shelter at an inn as he lifted the boy into the warmth of the room that Christmas-tide? The kindly landlord cared for Edward Polehampton, fed and clothed him, until at last the lad was able to set out on the road to London. He went to seek his fortune, as so many boys have done throughout the centuries but, where many failed Edward Polehampton succeeded.

Having become a pupil of a London painter, Henry Lyne, he was admitted to the Painter Stainers' Company and remained an honoured member until his death.

Unfortunately, little of Edward Polehampton's work remains. Although he painted some portraits, his work was chiefly centred on panels of allegorical and heraldic design. Very often these were used on the magnificent coaches of that period. He took pupils of his own, and was also a printseller. He prospered and was able to buy property, thus adding to his wealth.

Edward Polehampton of the Parish of St Sepulchre, London, Citizen and Painter Stainer, made his will on the 27th day of July 1721, by which time his charitable buildings at Twyford were already in the course of erection and he made provision for them to be completed if he should die before that time.

The will stipulated that the school should house ten poor boys between the ages of eight and 15. Although a boy might leave before the age of 15 if it was thought desirable, no pupil could remain after that age as his place must be taken by another child. Each boy would receive £10 a year for clothing.

A master was to be appointed at a salary of £40 a year, preferably a suitable minister of the Church of England who could also officiate at the chapel where divine service would be held every Sunday morning and afternoon. The boys were to attend the sermons preached at both services.

The benefactor accepted that the minister might not wish to act also as schoolmaster: in this case £10 would be deducted from his salary and paid to a suitable man who would reside in the schoolmaster's house. In either event, the master's income could be supplemented by taking in boarders in addition to the charity scholars.

Four trustees were appointed – the vicar of St Sepulchre, London, the vicar of St Nicholas, Hurst, and the vicar of St Mary's, Reading. These three trustees were forever; the fourth, Dr William Skelton of Doctors' Commons, London, was appointed for his natural life.

No mention of a wife was made in the will, although it would seem that Edward Polehampton was reunited with some members of his family during his lifetime for money was left to his nieces, Elizabeth Feelot and Mary Humphreys. Another woman, Mrs Shore, also received a small legacy; possibly she was his housekeeper. The executors, John Ford of London, citizen and bricklayer; Roger Askew of London, citizen and Painter Stainer; and William Skelton of Doctors' Commons, received gifts for their trouble.

Edward Polehampton died in 1722 and in accordance with his wishes, was buried in the churchyard at St Nicholas' Church, Hurst. There was no church at Twyford at this time, and the school chapel must have been a blessing for those who wished to attend a service but found the long walk to Hurst too exhausting. Although the chapel was never consecrated it was in use until the present church was built in Twyford in 1846.

A new state school was built in 1888 but it bears the name of Polehampton School. Part of the charity school building remains to this day, opposite the private house which was once the Rose and Crown Inn. Did the donor choose the site of his school so that it was in the shadow of the hostelry? The charity still exists and is administered for the benefit of needy children.

Perhaps one day the true answer will be found, and the reason for Polehampton's charity known for certain, but it will be difficult to replace the story of a landlord's kindness which brought such benefit to the boys of Twyford.

The Candle Auction

THE village of Aldermaston retains its old world charm in spite of being overshadowed by a giant atomic energy establishment. From the wrought iron gates of the 'Great House' which stands at one end of the village street, to the mellow brickwork of the Hind's Head Inn at the opposite end, the village atmosphere remains.

Along the street stand wisteria and rose-covered houses, the village lock-up is a grim reminder of harsher days, and a plaque on a garden wall calls attention to the place where in 1770 the village schoolmaster grew the first succulent Aldermaston, or William, pear.

It is fitting that such a village should be one of the last in England to retain an old custom – a candle auction. Indeed, the only other known candle auction (in Somerset) takes place but once in every 21 years so that Aldermaston can claim precedence in that its own auction is a triennial event.

The auction was first instituted in 1801 when Church Mead, a plot of land measuring 2 acres, 1 rod, 33 poles, was granted to the churchwardens of Aldermaston 'in compensation for their loss of goods and rights of common' after an enclosure act had deprived the church of its ancient right of pasturage on common land. As the church

119

had no cattle to graze on the newly acquired meadow, the wardens evidently decided to let the pasture to the highest bidder for a period of three years, and to use the rent received for purposes connected with their church. Ever since that first auction the practice has continued, with all the ceremony due to such an interesting occasion.

The first necessity is a tallow candle. The one that had been used for over a century having burned away in 1962, it was thought that a beeswax candle must be substituted at the next auction, but the lord of the manor came to the rescue and made a tallow candle which should last well into the next century.

A horsehoe nail is also needed. This type is used because the thin pin and heavy head should ensure that the nail drops correctly.

The lord of the manor inserts the pin into the tallow, one inch below the wick. The vicar's warden lights the candle, and by tradition, the vicar makes the first bid. As the candle burns the excitement grows. When the nail is seen to tilt the bidding becomes intense until the last moment when the nail falls to the table. Whoever makes the last call has the 'Church Acre' for the next three years at the annual rent of his bid. In 1801 the sum was £7. In 1974 it was £50.50, then an all time record being twice the amount of any previous sum offered for the meadow.

During this auction, at which I had the good fortune to be present, there was a most unusual development. The nail tilted and then lodged vertically into the hollow of the candle. The then churchwarden, the late Mr Bill Cox, who kindly told me the history of the auction, said that he had never before seen such a thing happen in all the years he had attended the ceremony. There was a moment's pause, then the bidding restarted with great rapidity until the nail finally dislodged and fell into the metal plate placed under the candle to ensure a resounding noise proclaiming that the auction is over. A local inhabitant was the highest bidder on that occasion and her horses grazed in the meadow by the river for the next three years. This was in contrast to the aftermath of the 1971 auction when an American succeeded in obtaining the Church Acre and on returning home had no use for the meadow.

Mr Cox's thirteenth attendance at the auction in 1977 brought him the luck of becoming tenant for the first time, when he called £46 as the nail fell, but as he had no horse the previous tenant continued to graze her horses in the field.

In recent years the bids have increased. They reached a record £104 in 1986, dropped to £95 in 1989 and rose to a new record of £116 in 1992 when a local farmer added £1 to the previous bid of £115 just seconds before the nail fell with a clang.

Throughout the ceremony the churchwardens smoke their long clay pipes and a special rum punch is brewed for the occasion. After the nail has fallen the People's Warden rises to snuff the candle. Then the tallow candle and the horseshoe nail are safely returned to their respective boxes to await the passing of the next three years and the coming of that auspicious occasion, the Aldermaston Candle Auction.

The Legend of Hawthorn Hill

THIS is a tale of two men – one who shrugged away good fortune and another who grasped at opportunity and with a combination of adventure, hard work, and a fair share of good luck, found wealth in an unexpected place.

It's an old story, told in varying forms in far-flung places, but Hawthorn Hill in Berkshire can lay claim to being the true location for the legend – at least it had two necessary attributes, an ancient tumulus and a thorn tree.

The story tells of an innkeeper who kept The Woodman Inn in Hawthorn. However, he had a recurring dream in which he was advised to leave his home to travel to London Bridge where he would hear something to his advantage. Understandably, the man thought little of the message after the first dream but when it was twice repeated he felt that he should travel to London and visit London Bridge to determine whether there was any truth in the matter.

It was quite an undertaking in those far off days for there were no proper roads. The innkeeper had probably never left his home before, and the area around Hawthorn Hill was thickly wooded. Tales of footpads would be known to the host of a wayside inn where travellers called for a night's lodging rather than face the perils of passing through unknown territory after dark. The dream must have been very convincing to make him bundle up a few belongings and set off for London on such a hazardous journey.

At the time old London Bridge was bordered by shops. The Berkshire innkeeper paused to wonder at the unfamiliar sights when he finally reached his destination. As he was pondering on his next move he was approached by a shopkeeper who enquired if he could be of help to the bewildered stranger. The countryman replied that he was a newcomer to the city, then, encouraged by the friendliness of the shopkeeper, he related his strange dream. The Londoner was amazed when he heard the tale. This man had left his inn to travel unknown paths to London, all on account of a dream! He could not help but laugh at the foolishness of this country bumpkin and advised him to return home before ill befell him in the streets of the city. Then, struck by a strange coincidence, he said that he too had once experienced a similar dream in which he had been told to travel to a place called Hawthorn. He had been told that on arrival at this unknown place he must look for a hill on which grew an ancient thorn tree. If he dug underneath the tree he would find a pot of gold. The shopkeeper laughed. What nonsense it all was. As if he was going to leave his shop on such a crazy errand.

Nonsense indeed agreed the innkeeper, who could hardly conceal his excitement. He thanked the London man for his good advice and said he would return home and forget the whole thing. He hurried back to Hawthorn because he knew full well where a thorn tree grew on the top of a hill, a tumulus in fact; just the place to find hidden treasure. When he reached his inn again he grabbed a spade and rushed off to the mound. It was not easy, digging down into the hard ground but he worked away and at last his spade struck the side of a pot. The dream came true – the pot was full of gold!

Legend does not relate if the innkeeper had a wife and family, but if he did they must have been delighted at the prospect of sharing his new-found wealth. However, their pleasure would have been shortlived. Alas, it was a case of 'easy come, easy go'. The innkeeper lived well and entertained his friends lavishly. The gold dwindled and went. Only the old pot stood on the shelf, a reminder of the prophetic dream.

One day two scholars from Oxford called at the inn for refreshment. They saw the pot and inquired if they might examine it more closely. A strange inscription round the rim had attracted their notice. The innkeper lifted it down from the shelf and handed it to the scholars. He said that he had often wondered about the lettering but he could not decipher the inscription. His guests studied it well and gave him the translation:

Beneath the place where this pot stood
There is another twice as good.

The innkeeper looked at the scholars in bewildered amazement. Surely there could not be another pot! Could his luck really be this good? Once more the innkeeper took his spade to dig deeper into the mound. Once more he had the good fortune to strike the side of a pot with the spade and sure enough there was an identical pot – except for one thing, this one had no inscription. His hands trembled as he lifted it from the ground and hurried back to the inn. As the golden coins tumbled on to the table he vowed he would be a wiser man this time and handle his riches with more care. This was his final chance – the uninscribed jar told of no further treasure. He was as good as his word, although he still welcomed travellers to his inn so that they could find comfort and shelter within its walls, but it was no longer called The Woodman but aptly renamed The Money Pot.